URBAN ELDERS

Family, Work,
and Welfare
among Boston's Aged,
1890–1950

Brian Gratton

URBAN ELDERS

Family, Work,
and Welfare
among Boston's Aged,
1890–1950

Temple University Press

Philadelphia

This publication has been supported by the National Endowment for the Humanities, a federal agency which supports the study of such fields as history, philosophy, literature, and languages.

REF
HQ
1064
.U6
M398
1986

R00514 26615

Temple University Press, Philadelphia 19122
Copyright © 1986 by Temple University. All rights reserved
First published 1986
Printed in the United States of America

Library of Congress Cataloging-in-Publication Data

Gratton, Brian.
Urban elders.

Bibliography: p.
Includes index.
1. Old age–History–20th century.
2. Aged–Massachusetts–Boston–Family relationships–History–20th century.
3. Aged–Employment–Massachusetts–Boston–History–20th century.
4. Old age assistance–Massachusetts–Boston–History–20th century.
I. Title.
HQ1064.U6M398   1985   305.2'6'0974461   85-14791
ISBN 0-87722-390-4

To Pat and Lorene

Contents

Figure and Tables

Acknowledgments

The late 1970s hardly promised much to students venturing careers in history. At Boston University the members of a very talented graduate student class prompted one another to valor if not discretion. Several of these friends have now been compelled to abandon research careers, a loss to American scholarship. In the faculty, Robert Bruce and Aileen Kraditor taught me very different but equally important standards. Arnold Offner, my director, saved the bark from the rocks on more than one occasion, and he and his wife, Ellen, remain trusted advisors.

Louis Lowy, professor in the School of Social Work, and J. Michael Ross, then professor of sociology, encouraged me to take the difficult step of learning another discipline. Both men cared more about their students then their own careers, and I am indebted to them for introducing me to social science. An imperfect student, I learned something of that craft while a postdoctoral fellow at Case Western Reserve University, largely because of the consummate training given me by Marie Haug, now professor emirita of sociology. David Van Tassel, professor of history in Western Reserve, proved that he deserves his reputation as a patron of fledgling historians; such teachers and friends, along with the Cleveland Symphony Orchestra, made my fellowship at Case a grand experience.

For that opportunity, funded by the National Institute on Aging, and for the support of the original research for this book by the Administration on Aging (Grant no. 90-A-797), I have good reason to applaud the welfare state. Without grants from our government, I could not have followed this profession, much less pursued this research. Since I was encouraged to express freely my professional judgment, the point of view and opinions stated in this book do not necessarily represent the position of these federal agencies. I also acknowledge permission granted by the Rogerson House, the Home for Aged Women, and Long Island Hospital to examine their records.

I finished the book at Arizona State University, an institution that supports its researchers; in the department of history, chaired by Frederick Giffin, I found the environment all assistant professors wish for. Some of the ideas presented in Chapter IV previously appeared in *Older Women: Issues and Prospects*, edited by Elizabeth W. Markson (Lexington, Mass., 1983), and a revised form of Chapter I has been published in *Growing Old in America*, 3d edition, edited by Beth Hess and Elizabeth Markson (New Brunswick, N.J., 1985). An anonymous reader for Temple University Press made very important contributions to the final revisions of the manuscript.

Academics are among the most satisfied of workers, for reasons we find rather obscure when we view our paychecks. Certainly one part of our recompense is the discovery of a community of scholars who live up to the ideal of collegiality. Linda Belgrave, Tom Cole, David Ekerdt, Rachel Fuchs, Janet Golden, Bill Graebner, Carole Haber, Beth Luey, John Myles, Walker Pollard, Jill Quadagno, Eric Schneider, Alvin Schorr, and Lynn Weiner—colleagues drawn from six disciplines—read and reread the manuscript, often not agreeing with the argument, but always reading cheerfully, and always without quarter.

My father is a handsome Irishman, now 85, full of expert chronicles in fine English, and still quicker of wit than his son. He has contributed to every aspect of this book. My mother's family homesteaded eastern New Mexico; beset by drought, they went bust and moved to town. I greatly profited from their bankruptcy: in her keen sensitivity to brushstroke on canvas, to landscape, and to family, my mother enriched all her children. As my grandmother used to say, I drew to a good pair, and I dedicate this book to my parents.

URBAN ELDERS

Family, Work,
and Welfare
among Boston's Aged,
1890–1950

Introduction

As an aging nation, we fear the cost of retirement and are uneasy about future rapport between the young and the old. These concerns provoke interest in the history of old age: how have older people come to be a dependent population and a threat to social and economic stability?

During the last decade an energetic group of historians sought an answer to this question. Reaching back across the nineteenth century and into the colonial era, they attempted to determine the critical period for the transformation of attitudes toward old age, the point at which the cultural view of older men and women shifted from respect to disdain. The preeminence they gave to attitude as a historical event and causal force reflects partly a contemporary obsession with "ageism," partly the nature of causal thinking in American historiography, and partly their research findings.

Attitudinal histories are valuable in unveiling the long record of prejudice toward old age, and historians have developed a rightful indignation about the crude structuralism of modernization theory. However, their reaction to this theory led them to unwarranted conclusions about the influence of attitudes. It is true that social scientists have blithely relied on ahistorical structural models to explain the reduced circumstances of our older citizens. But in rejecting the pretensions of a bad structural explanation, most historians merely assigned causal powers to attitudes rather than proving them.

The failure to prove the causal effects of attitudes invites a new investigation of structural data. William Graebner's trenchant and provocative analysis of the Social Security Act in his *A History of Retirement* convinced me that the crucial period of change lay in the twentieth century. The availability of rich stores of evidence in a single urban center led to the course of research laid out in this book. From the beginning, structural issues attracted me: I studied the demography, labor force activity, and welfare of Boston's elderly population, defining that population as people 60 or 65 and over. My intent has been to test whether structural factors could help to explain the history of the twentieth-century aged. I have not attempted to write a history of attitudes toward old age in this period and place, primarily because recent attitudinal accounts largely ignore structural evidence, and secondly because attitudinal approaches often preclude an understanding of the lives of large numbers of people whose "attitudes" are never written down. Perhaps an attitudinal account would lead to different conclusions than the ones presented here, but that task remains to others.

Nor have I attempted to write a book about old age in the United States at this time (a book already written several times over by other historians). I chose Boston, as a prototypical area. By the early twentieth century, it already represented the urban, postindustrial, and welfare-oriented society that we associate with our own time. By 1950 the city had witnessed fully the transformation by which old age becomes a social rather than simply a familial or personal concern. Although conditions differed in other areas, many cities mirrored Boston's circumstances in the first half of the century, and the nation was moving toward this urban life, much to the discomfort of many of its inhabitants. Boston offered an opportunity to examine intimately what happened to old people in this process.

The great advantage in focusing attention on one area lay in the clarity and consistency of the data: demographic characteristics were not obscured by the inclusion of rural populations and different racial groups; labor force statistics were always drawn from an industrial and postindustrial sector; and welfare for the aged was, from the beginning, an important local issue, not something imposed by the federal government in 1935. What emerged from the research was the profile of a struggle over a new system of age relations, a struggle in which the needs of the aged only occasionally played a part.

The striking consequences of this conflict make it clear that the history of American old age must be divided into three parts: preindustrial, industrial, and post–New Deal. The singular finding of the research was that before the New Deal, even in an advanced urban area, the average older man worked. After the 1930s, older men left the labor force in droves. Their labor force participation between 1890 and 1930 was extensive and relatively stable. Each cohort of older workers seemed to experience difficulty in qualifying for new occupations, while enjoying security in older ones. (Older women workers incurred an additional liability because years of training in housework found little reward in the labor market.) The conventional picture of an increasingly marginal, outmoded, and impoverished older population—a vision promoted in both modernization theory and attitudinal alternatives—fails to explain this evidence. In Boston, not only did most older men work, but there is little evidence that the average older worker fell into menial trades or lost occupational prestige.

Given these conditions, the precipitous decline in labor force participation among older men after 1930 was even more astonishing. By 1950 less than two-fifths of Boston's older men remained in the labor force. I conclude that the old age benefits of a new welfare state were primarily responsible for the permanent decline in labor force activity. New Deal retirement instruments removed the aged from the labor force at a stroke. The result was a remarkable social transformation whose full effects we are experiencing today: within 20 years the proportion of Boston's older population dependent on younger persons for some form of public welfare increased from 6 percent to more than 50 percent. Generally seen as a benevolent response to a long process of decline in the status of the aged, the Social Security Act in fact precipitated the exclusion of older workers.

If the old age benefits of the welfare state cannot be explained simply by the assumption that old people needed help, what are their origins? Demographic conditions reveal one important source of popular support for New Deal programs. The slow pace of overall demographic change in Boston disguised radical changes among certain subpopulations. Immigration slowed the aging of the aggregate population, but particular ethnic groups aged suddenly. Such groups had good reason to look to the state for relief from the burden of caring for large numbers of elderly poor, the great majority of whom were widows dependent on their children.

By 1950 even the aggregate population was experiencing the consequences of long-term demographic change: the number of children available to support older people had diminished greatly. From the late nineteenth century to 1950, however, Boston's older people continued to rely on the family household for lodging and support. Therefore the extraordinary isolation of older people in contemporary America—a very large proportion now live outside the family household—has occurred only since 1950. Older women, the chief burden on families before the New Deal, now constitute welfare's chief beneficiaries and the population most isolated from the family household. It seems unlikely that normative changes have suddenly led the generations to live apart. Across the century, the rising probability that an adult Bostonian would have to support an aged parent made the advantages of the welfare state perfectly plain, and a steady income for older people sufficient to support separate residence had attractions for both generations.

Before old age benefits made such living arrangements possible, a sizable minority of older men and women were "covertly" dependent; that is, they relied upon their families for support. However, since the movement for social security* used the overtly or publicly dependent aged as symbols of the need for new welfare programs, the history of these older persons might help explain the origins of the welfare state. To this end, I use case studies of public and private charities to explore the nature of overt dependency among older women and men. I contrast a dominant private charity approach, exemplified in two prominent old age homes, with the public welfare system's almshouse and outdoor relief divisions. In these examples of public and private relief, I seek first to present a clear account of the old people who did not share in the general success of Boston's aged population, and then to comprehend the reasons for their dependency in old age.

Further, I believe that the political history of social security needs rescuing. The circumstances of life for the majority of Boston's aged suggest that the Social Security Act was hardly inevitable. The campaign for state welfare for the aged provoked a class and ethnic struggle, deep, intense, and divisive. The pre–New Deal welfare system was certainly politically charged. A private welfare network, dominated by native Protestants, sought to impose a punitive, highly restricted welfare program on the working classes. In providing special private charity, Yankees violated their own

* In this book, "social security" refers generally to governmental programs to assist the elderly, while "Social Security" applies specifically to the federal legislation of 1935.

welfare code, but for a select few. They hoped to help the ruined upper classes of the city, but they settled for clerks and domestics, who proved their worthiness by demonstrating Yankee ancestry. Immigrant Catholics were compelled to seek relief from a poor church system or from public sources. The most unfortunate and isolated among them ended up in the city almshouse. Here they endured an ignominious fate, usually after years of hard work rather than indolence.

Whether the clients of private or public welfare, blue collar or white collar, Irish or Yankee, overtly dependent old people shared a paucity of family members. Lack of family was the principal cause of institutionalization. In itself, this fact only confirms historically what social gerontologists maintain at present. But the identification of the family factor in overt dependency has implications for *covert* dependency—that is, dependency within the family—and the pressures this burden may have exerted toward the development of the welfare state. Irish and Italian families in Boston struggled to avoid the almshouse, at great material and psychological cost. Even if the old father or mother kept at home did not need nursing care, the strain on family time and resources could be great. Since the private Yankee charities disliked the very idea of relief and loathed its disbursement to immigrants, the natural avenue to lighten the family burden was to seek an expansion of public welfare.

Success crowned this course. During the 1920s, as Irish politicians solidified their control of the city, dramatic increases in aid for the elderly appeared in Boston's public welfare records. Both the number of beneficiaries and the real value of relief grants rose during this decade. No compelling evidence suggests that these increases resulted from rising dependency among the aged; rather, public welfare officials seem to have redefined dependency in a more generous manner, giving public monies to elders once thought undeserving.

With the passage of a state old age assistance bill in 1930 (legislation resisted by the Yankee social welfare elite), Boston provided still more elderly people with benefits, although the average benefit level did not increase. In the mid-1930s, both the state and the federal governments exerted more influence over old age assistance, and Washington contributed additional funds. By 1950 nearly 30 percent of Boston's elderly received public relief, and an additional 25 percent received Social Security insurance. Public welfare, which once aided a small minority of Boston's aged and their families, now made up the basic bill of fare.

Evidence from beneficiary case records and official documents of Boston's welfare system warrants the inference that *covert*, intrafamilial dependency in the ethnic, working-class communities of Boston provoked the momentous transformation from familial to institutional exchange between generations. Transfers of support between generations had once been mediated through the family; by 1950 they occurred through the offices of the welfare state. As Charles Trout has demonstrated in *Boston, the Great Depression, and the New Deal*, the ascendancy of Irish political power in Boston led directly to the unseating of the Yankee elite's social welfare officials, who had disparaged the immigrant, distrusted the applicant, and detested relief. The old age pension movement, which succeeded in 1930 in forcing a Republican legislature to expand state welfare for the aged, relied on working-class, ethnic constituencies for its political strength. Seeking security for their own old age and assistance for the elders in their families and communities, working-class leaders demanded a state pension financed by a tax on the middle and upper classes. In the welfare legislation of the 1930s and 1940s, they made significant progress toward that goal.

The social impact was as dramatic as the dire prophecies of the Yankee elite had foretold. Social security in Boston immediately resulted in what conservative critics now assert is its national effect: an unprecedented reconstruction of the relationship between the state and its citizens and the relationship between young and old. As the pivot in the social transformation whose results we question today, the welfare state influences the experience of both the old and their children. We may approve or disapprove of these consequences, but we should carefully attend to the history of their origins.

Chapter I
The History
of American
Old Age

Until the last decade, little empirical research had been done on the history of old age in America. Most social scientists applied the basic tenets of modernization theory to the elderly, arguing that industrialization and urbanization had impoverished older men and women and reduced their status. But recent historical work has shaken confidence in modernization theory. Historians maintain that attitudinal rather than structural forces have been most important in effecting change in the status of older people. Whereas modernization theory explained the history of the aged in terms of structural differences between traditional and modern societies, the new historians view *ageism* as an independent force and see a culture's attitudes toward old age as the crucial influence. The significance of this debate goes beyond academic concerns, since each interpretation explains quite differently how the elderly came to be a "social problem" in our own time. Because the major factors of change that these schools identify receive empirical evaluation in this book, their respective arguments deserve preliminary review.

The Critique of
Modernization Theory

The application of modernization theory to the American elderly stemmed from early twentieth-century concern over poverty and dependency: it was presumed that the shift from an agricultural to an industrial economy drove older Americans into dependency. This interpretation of the decline in the status of the aged had intuitive roots: it appealed to common sense, nostalgia, and fear of industrialization and urbanization. The first advocates of old age pensions seized upon "modernization"—though they did not call it that— as a ready explanation for the pitiful state of the elderly in industrial America and as a justification for government relief.[1] In the 1950s modernization flowered as a general scholarly theory when American intellectuals, faced with an emerging Third World, sought a Western model to explain the process of economic development.[2] Reference to modernization theory among social gerontologists soon reached the level of dogma.[3]

Those who applied modernization theory to the aged contrasted modern industrial societies with stable agricultural ones.[4] In the latter the aged enjoyed relative economic security and high status. Their good fortune followed from several conditions. First, landed property represented power in agricultural economies. The old tended to control such property; hence, they maintained authority over a needy younger generation. Second, the family was the unit of economic organization, and the property rights of the older members gave them a direct and forceful influence over the lives of the younger members. Since the family was extended, a broad patriarchal authority guaranteed security in old age. Third, as farmers who controlled their own employment, old people continued to perform a useful and valued work role. Finally, in such societies the aged were repositories of wisdom born of long experience; they passed on to the younger generation skills, knowledge, and traditions (including the veneration of age).

Conversely, according to modernization theory, in advanced societies the aged experience reduced economic circumstances and status. Landed property no longer represents the major source of wealth and power in an industrial economy, and the family no longer serves as the unit of economic organization. Under these conditions, the aged lose control over younger family members. The extended family disintegrates into nuclear units more suitable for the geographic and economic mobility needed in industrial societies. As workers who sell their labor power, old people have no advantage over other workers, and since they may in fact be judged inferior, they suffer high unemployment. The aged lose both claims to high status: income and the work role. In a literate population, education among the young exceeds that of the aged, and the communication of information, skills, and tradition does not depend on the old timers. Finally, as a result of these changes and a demographic transition, large numbers of the elderly become impoverished and dependent, visible symbols of their age group's reduced status.

Criticism of modernization theory grew first out of a general distaste for the abrupt break posited between traditional and modern societies.[5] Historians maintained that there were great differences among traditional societies, and some social gerontologists argued that even in modern nations culture might be more important than economic conditions.[6] But the most striking criticism sprang from the discovery that the nuclear household constituted the dominant family form in preindustrial Western societies.[7] Thus, the aged could not have exercised power through an extended family. Since social gerontologists had begun to find that the aged in modern societies maintained close contact with their kin, a sharp break between past and present seemed unlikely. Historians also found evidence of strong hostility toward the aged in traditional societies.[8] American historians threw even more suspicion on structural interpretations by locating a shift from veneration toward vilification of the aged apparently independent of industrialization and urbanization.[9]

These criticisms exposed the weaknesses in the broad and vague generalizations characteristic of modernization theory, attacked the structural dynamic at its heart, and focused attention on the influence of ageism in the history of the elderly. Nonetheless, a review of the new historical literature suggests that its conclusions remain at best incomplete. The new history provides no sustained analysis of the control exercised by the aged over land, business, skills, and wealth in agricultural societies. The anthropology of old age and the new history itself reveal that a variety of cultures exhibit a universal pattern: where older people control resources necessary to satisfy the needs of younger persons, the elders' status will generally be high.[10]

Such control exists most often in societies where property may be privately held. Family tensions and intergenerational conflicts—often cited as proof that the elderly were not well regarded in the past[11]—actually reflect the power of older people in the economic inheritance system. Historical studies of peasant Europe and colonial America provide similar evidence of the authority available to elders in landowning economies.[12] Property-based status relied only indirectly on age but had obvious implications for age relations. The natural consequence of growing older was to come into possession of the means of production and thereby to exercise some control over one's environment and over younger generations.

We would fully expect that an economic transition of the magnitude of industrialization, which undermined the previous economic system and its age relations, would have a direct effect on the place of the aged in society. But the new histories of aging in America explicitly reject this logic: they see the structural change from farm to factory as of little consequence. Rather, they connect the decline in the status of the elderly to an independent force, ageism. Cultural attitude is judged to be more important than structure.

The New History of
the American Elderly

David Hackett Fischer was the first to argue that American history demonstrated the failure of modernization theory because the decline in the status of the aged occurred *before* "industrialization, urbanization, and the growth of mass education— . . . [before] 'modernization' in the ordinary meaning of the term." Fischer proposed that a period of exaltation of the aged (1607–1820) was shattered by a "new set of ideas," resulting in a "revolution in age relations" (1770–1820). American society was from this point set on a "straight and stable" course toward the triumph of gerontophobia, the fear of old age.[13]

After initial enthusiasm, most scholars have come to doubt Fischer's analysis.[14] Fischer's reliance on urban sources provided little proof of transformation in the lives of the mass of men and women in America, who, as farmers, played their parts in a local, familial, and traditional network. This distinction was perfectly expressed in a remark made by the Reverend William Bentley of Salem, Massachusetts, when visiting rural Andover in 1793. Bentley noted that the country people gathered to dance "in classes due to their ages, not with regard to their [economic] condition as in the Seaport Towns."[15]

In fact, Fischer unintentionally supports the theory he criticized. In a penetrating account of seventeenth- and eighteenth-century New England, he finds that this society's literature cautioned the young to venerate their elders as wise and as specially favored by God. The aged often served in high office; owners of property, they exercised great authority over their sons and daughters, to the point that "land was an instrument of generational politics" and "youth was the hostage of age." Indeed, the high status of the elderly led many people to report themselves older than they were: in two large censuses taken in 1776 and 1787 (in Maryland

and Connecticut respectively), the observable biases in the reporting of age run in the opposite direction from all known modern censuses, showing a clear *preference* for greater age.[16] Instead of excess numbers of persons stating that they were 39, or 49, excess numbers report themselves 41 or 51. This is a most exciting finding. The bias toward youth is so pronounced in our time that we must assume that Americans' view of age was utterly different in the late eighteenth century. No more telling evidence exists in the social history of the aged.

When we combine this evidence with other studies of the power and security enjoyed by the property-owning elderly in America's agricultural, family-based economy,[17] the picture of a "traditional" world appears remarkably like that proposed in modernization theory. A father in colonial Virginia directs in his will: "Sons Michael, Rupert, and Matthew are to obey their mother and follow her orders or they are not to get their land."[18] The pattern can be found in other studies of old age, which find that respect for the aged in early New England reveals a "gerontocratic society founded . . . 'by patriarchs, which gave office to its elders, not its youth, and believed in hierarchy.'"[19]

Fischer's unintended confirmation of one claim of modernization theory was not followed by a persuasive case for sudden social revolution in age relations in the period 1770–1820. Old people's loss of status in the heavily populated northeastern area in the eighteenth century occurred because average farm holdings diminished and the powers of inheritance could not be exercised: "During most of the eighteenth century scarcity increased and the older matrix of values sustaining respect for the aged withered."[20] However, this long process began anew in each area of frontier settlement.[21] It remains the more reasonable hypothesis to view the decline in the status of the aged as a fairly steady trend across the nineteenth century, a consequence of the relative decline of agriculture in the American economy.

Nonetheless, this remains a hypothesis, for little solid evidence exists regarding the crucial transition period of the nineteenth century. Fischer relies on an impressionistic reading of literature. His use of Whitman's poetry, for example, is both selective and inaccurate, and his review of a number of literary works proves only that one can find negative references to the elderly in a survey of American literature and popular culture between 1800 and 1970.[22] Rather more light has been shed on the nineteenth century by W. Andrew Achenbaum, whose major history of old age in America also stresses attitudinal change over structural forces. Again, industrialization and urbanization are found to be insufficient to explain declines in status because, in Achenbaum's argument, they occurred both before and after the onset of the degradation of old age.[23] In an exhaustive survey of middle-class literature since 1790, Achenbaum found ambivalence toward the aged at all times, but a relatively favorable climate in the antebellum period. In the late nineteenth century, however, he locates a decisive break, a broad denial of the aged and the emergence of a cult of youth, with hostility to age visible in medical texts and in evaluations of the aged worker.[24] Many scholars now agree with Achenbaum's dating of the attitudinal shift toward old age, and hence with a periodization that divides the history of the aged into two parts, with the critical period occurring at the end of the nineteenth century. Achenbaum's argument that the negative shift occurred independently of structural change (that is, change in the aged's occupational and demographic circumstances) depends on an analysis of labor force participation rates, to which we will return.

Carole Haber agrees with Achenbaum that the 1880s and 1890s brought forth a new order that oppressed the aged, but she emphasizes the consequences of a growing tendency among doctors to equate old age with sickness.[25] In her critical history of geriatrics, Haber notes its simultaneous reliance on advances in scientific medicine and on cultural prejudices. By the late nineteenth century, the result was the segregation of the aged in a medical category that labeled old age as sickness but offered no cure. Haber finds the same emphasis on the classification and segregation of the aged as obviously dependent in studies of the labor market, institutionalization, and charity work. She connects new discriminatory practices directly to structural change in economic and familial relations, and her recognition of the reciprocal relationship between structural poverty among older people and the bureaucratic response to it among the "helping professions" greatly enhances our understanding of the origins of ageism. Haber argues that a new concept of the work cycle, terminated by the novel status of retirement, was the result first of an excessive labor supply and second of the tendency of various elites to emphasize the incapacity of the aged. However, her labor supply argument does not fit well with employers' favorable attitudes toward immigration at the turn of the century, and her treatment of retirement, while sensitive to the negative effects of pensions as a substitute for work, fails to address the most obvious question: what proportion of workers was actually affected by retirement programs? Pension plans and mandatory retirement applied to very few workers as late as 1930. It is doubtful that mandatory retirement has ever affected a large proportion of American workers, yet most of the new historians use any instance of it as proof of the general downgrading of the aged.[26] Nonetheless, Haber joins the historian William Graebner in rightly emphasizing the issue of retirement. Although perhaps not so significant at the turn of the century as they claim, the eventual broad implementation of this idea in the Social Security Act of 1935 rewrote age relations for the nation.

Historians of the family have focused on the composition of households and the timing of life events. Research by Tamara Hareven and others has given us a new understanding of the typical experience of the aged, has stressed the absence of sharp breaks between middle age and old age during the nineteenth century, and has shown that the long "empty nest" period for older couples is a phenomenon that has become prevalent only in our time.[27] Daniel Scott Smith and his colleagues have taken national samples of the aged American population from the 1880 and 1900 manuscript censuses.[28] The samples record the somewhat limited information provided for individuals, as well as data regarding the families and neighborhoods of aged persons. Although the decision to take every aged person found on systematically chosen pages may bias the sample toward aged persons who live in proximity—that is, married couples—the device does allow the investigators to gather interesting data on kinship, occupation, and ethnicity in the neighborhoods of the aged.

Smith's design precludes analysis of change over time, but he argues that "change in the family status of the older population has been slow historically, with most of the change occurring only in recent decades."[29] In essence Smith's assumption is a rejection of modernization theory's contention that industrialization and urbanization undermined the family networks of the aged.[30] These demographic studies have given us an informative description of old age at the turn of the century: older people were relatively independent; they tended to head households or to be spouses of the head; and the men among them had high labor force participation rates. Smith's findings support the continuity of life that Hareven has emphasized and underscore the historical independence of older people. Nonetheless, in 1900, 35 to 40 percent of those over 65 lived in extended households, many of which they headed.[31] When an older person was not the head or spouse of the head, he or, more often, she lived with a child. Thus, the family composed "the welfare institution for old people." Smith does not believe that this practice was a product of "economic necessity," despite the fact that the coresidents were generally aged women.[32]

His implication is that attitudes influenced decisions about coresidence. In the most recent examination of these data, Smith is skeptical of interpretations that view recent dramatic declines in coresidence as a product of the welfare state or of shifts in the composition of the aged population. He asserts that rising income since World War II cannot explain recent declines in coresidence of children and aged parents, since in 1900 he found the lowest level of coresidence in poorer families and high levels in the middle classes. Smith concludes that some change of *values* must have occurred.[33]

Industrial Capitalism and the Older Worker

Until quite recently, twentieth-century histories of the elderly focused on, and were influenced by, the early reform movements that addressed the poverty of old people.[34] Achenbaum's twentieth-century material rewards the reader by summarizing Social Security policy, but it is marred by a failure to address the negative effects of New Deal legislation, especially on older workers.[35] An optimistic view of the mid-nineteenth-century aged worker leads Achenbaum to the conclusion that the decline in status came all in a rush in the twentieth century, propelled by "negative attitudes" toward the aged. Since "ideas . . . have a life of their own," the rise of ageism after the Civil War was not directly connected to "*actual* demographic, occupational, and economic" conditions. Instead, like Fischer's "deep change," but a hundred years later, an attitudinal shift set in motion a general decline in the status of the elderly.[36]

The Social Security Act is thus interpreted as a legislative "solution" to the problems of the aged. In *Shades of Gray*, Achenbaum argues that such legislation showed "an un-

precedented concern for the elderly by the federal government."[37] Again, he emphasizes the role of ideas and values
in the evolution of national policy.

Achenbaum's ideational argument rests on a particular
treatment of the aged labor force, one that has prompted
agreement among a number of scholars.[38] Achenbaum maintains, contrary to conventional structural theory, that nineteenth-century industrialization did not undermine the position of the aged. Instead, the attitudinal shift late in the
century set in motion an inevitable decline in the status of
the older worker, subsequently expressed by declining labor
force activity from 1900 to the present.[39]

Since reliable labor force participation data are not available for the nineteenth century, a good test of his proposition
cannot presently be devised. But Achenbaum's estimates of
steady and high nineteenth-century participation rates are
internally inconsistent and unlikely to be sustained in future
research.[40] In addition, most scholars misread the declines
in participation in the twentieth century. Although participation rates fell before 1930, they did so at a slow pace. It
can be shown that no relative declines occurred before 1940
for older agricultural workers and only slight ones for industrial workers. The source of the general fall in participation rates lies in the relationship *between* these sectors.
As the economy industrialized, the relatively low participation of older men in industrial work began to dominate
their general participation rates. This is exactly as structural
theory would have it. But still more intriguing is the replacement of this continued but slow decline in participation with a precipitous drop between 1930 and the present.
Given the establishment and expansion of social security
programs during this period, it seems likely, as many economists presently maintain, that old age relief benefits acted
as a magnet, drawing older workers out of the labor force.
Thus, rather than being a benevolent response to the inu-

tility of the older worker, government legislation appears to be *creating* useless workers.

Nineteenth-century labor force participation rates probably exhibited the same slow decline found in the early twentieth century as the shift from an agricultural to a non-agricultural economy proceeded. Farms and the small-scale enterprises that evolved from skilled trades favored the aged, who often controlled access to skill and capital.[41] But the development of large-scale industry undercut these advantages, diminishing older people's capacity to control their own employment as well as that of the sons and daughters on whom they then depended in old age. Industrialization reduced, although it did not eliminate, the value of their bequests.[42] Even those elderly people who farmed sometimes lost to industrial cities the children who they had hoped would honor and work for them in the traditional way. The end of the nineteenth century witnessed a great transition in the industrial work force, the destruction of the capacity of senior workers to control production, and the spread of scientific management, through which employers stripped away the advantages of older workers.[43]

Even so, little evidence has been produced to show that the position of the aged within the industrial sector declined more dramatically during the early twentieth century than in the nineteenth. Scattered findings in both periods indicate a fairly consistent and stable pattern of high participation rates and some accumulation of wealth for the majority, and downward mobility, poverty, and dependency on children for a minority.[44] Since the debate among economists concerns not whether, but how much, social security reduces the participation of older workers, historians would be well advised to consider carefully what kind of labor force was emerging before such welfare measures were instituted. Before 1935, most older men remained in the labor force, and the proportion of aged men among workers steadily increased. Yet less than two decades after the Social Security Act, most older men were retired.

The origins and consequences of this momentous act have been insightfully examined by William Graebner.[45] Graebner's revisionist view of the New Deal leads to a powerful critique of conventional interpretations of legislation and of the periodization of the history of old age. His argument is in one sense attitudinal: like Haber and Achenbaum, he locates the rise of a retirement concept harmful to the aged in the late nineteenth century. But Graebner's original contribution lies in his analysis of a series of twentieth-century experiments in retirement that, stimulated first by concern for efficiency and subsequently by fear of unemployment, led directly to the Social Security Act. Exploring the history of railroad retirement in the early thirties and the inner workings of the Committee on Economic Security, which drafted Social Security legislation, Graebner concludes that the 1935 act was a "piece of unemployment legislation," "designed within a labor market context" to make room for young workers by the "removal" of their aged competitors.[46] This has been said before, but never with such penetrating effect.

Some reservations about Graebner's account are necessary. Social Security and the state pensions that preceded it were popular measures, opposed by powerful elites who receive little attention in Graebner's work. State pensions were not the product of efficiency experts or retirement experimenters, but of the working class, which underwrote the long and difficult campaigns.[47] Still, the architects of policy in Roosevelt's Committee on Economic Security did argue that retirement would make room for younger workers. In this strategy they were joined by powerful political allies, the Townsendites, a movement of older people and their allies who demanded government pensions for old people, predicted their positive consequences for unemployment rates, and threatened to remove from office those legislators who demurred.⁴⁸ From this perspective emerges a critical insight: the Social Security Act created dependency as much as it reduced it.

Since Graebner's work, which relied so heavily on the actions of a state manipulated by corporate elites, a number of sociologists have taken up a similar theme, with a corresponding focus on the Social Security Act. Interested in testing theories of the bureaucratic state as an independent historical agent, these social scientists divorce themselves from conventional accounts of the origins of welfare, which emphasize demographic, structural factors. John Myles argues that the democratic state constitutes an arena in which the working class has struggled to secure a retirement wage free from market criteria, at times in concert with the interests of capitalist elites, but now with successes so great that these elites predict fiscal crisis unless public entitlements are reduced. Jill Quadagno maintains that the New Deal government played an independent role in responding to the failure of the private sector to establish a pension system, but functioned primarily to mediate among a variety of economic interest groups in determining the provisions of the Social Security Act. Since Quadagno, along with sociologists like Theda Skocpol, has argued that the working class did not actively campaign for state welfare (in contradistinction to the European experience), she also believes that the act did not respond well to working-class needs. Skocpol and Ann Shola Orloff give the "state" its greatest role in the drama of welfare; industrialization, ideology, and working-class or capitalist demands, while not irrelevant, are insufficient explanations for the development of welfare. State structure—that is, the internal organization of government and the attitudes of political elites—determines the timing and form of welfare programs.⁴⁹

Although the emphasis on the state in this research offers a new, if somewhat mystical, approach, historians have shown little interest in it. Most of the new histories view the Social Security Act as reactive legislation rather than as a formative event upon which the periodization of the history of American old age rests. Having exposed the weaknesses of modernization theory, the new historians of old age have rejected structural arguments in favor of culture: change in values, the rise of ageism. As this review suggests, attitudinal explanations may be as inadequate as the modernization theory they replaced, and the collapse of modernization theory does not discredit all structural interpretations.

In the debate between structural and attitudinal analyses, certain issues have taken center stage. The demographic and familial characteristics of older people, poverty and welfare policy, and labor force activity provoke the greatest interest in recent literature, all with good reason. These factors figure prominently in the current crisis over age relations, and their historical development demands our attention. These are the factors that this book addresses.

Chapter II
Gender, Ethnicity, and Family: The Demography of Boston's Elderly

Although Boston's demographic history occasionally differs markedly from national and rural patterns, it parallels urban trends. The aging of the urban population, exceedingly slow until about 1920, proceeded rapidly during the next 30 years. Immigration was an especially important demographic factor in many American cities, first retarding the pace of aging, then accelerating it. Indeed, ethnicity is essential to understanding the nature of aging in places like Boston, where the foreign-born made up a majority of the elderly population.

Large cities also exhibited disproportionate numbers of aged women, and among these women, widows predominated. In Boston and other eastern urban areas, single females made up another large part of the older population. If the "problem" of old age had one symbolic representative in early twentieth-century Boston, the unmarried Irishwoman played the part.

In the larger sense, however, the problem of old age for all the United States stemmed from a falling birth rate. Between 1890 and 1950, the relative number of children who might assist the American elderly declined very rapidly. The imbalance between the number of the aged and the number of adult children put great pressure on families. A detailed examination of such "dependency ratios" and of the household composition of the elderly in Massachusetts indicates that the family tried to perform its welfare role as late as 1950. Therefore, unless attitudes toward family responsibility have changed very abruptly, normative change cannot explain the dramatic rise in recent years in the proportion of older people who live alone. The evidence suggests instead that Americans always preferred separate residence for the adult and aged generations but that, before the welfare state, families often were compelled to house aged parents, especially mothers. Families now take advantage of the welfare state's provision of funds for alternatives to coresidence. The ethnic, sexual, and proportionate characteristics of the aged population in Boston show that certain groups had good reason to seek the generous extension of old age benefits through the welfare state, since these spread the cost of supporting the elderly, and greatly reduced the risk of coresidence.

The Aged in Boston: Proportion, Nativity, and Marital Status

Table II-1 shows the percentage of Boston residents who were 65 and over between 1830 and 1950.[1] Less than 2 percent of the city in 1830, the aged had become almost one-tenth of its population in 1950. The rate of increase, however, varied greatly as is shown graphically in Figure II-1. It is plain that the population of nineteenth-century Boston matured very slowly. Between 1830 and 1875 the percentage of the city's population claimed by older Bostonians (65 and over) increased by slightly more than one percent, and, from 1875 to 1915, the rate of increase actually declined. The year 1915 marked a turning point in this process; after this year the population aged very rapidly. Between 1920 and 1930, the percentage of Boston's population that was 65 and over rose from 4.4 to 5.5 percent, a 25 percent increase in a single decade. Subsequent demographic aging

Gender, Ethnicity, and Family

Table II–1.

Men and Women 65 and Over as a Percentage of Population in Boston, in Massachusetts, and in the United States, 1830–1950

Census Year	Boston Total	Women	Men	Mass.	U.S.
1830	1.9[a]				
1840	1.8[a]				
1845	1.9[a]				
1850	1.9[a]				
1860	2.3[a]				
1875	3.2	3.6	2.7	5.0	
1885	3.8	4.3	3.3	5.5	
1890	3.8	4.3	3.3	5.4	3.9
1895	3.7	4.2	3.2	5.3	
1900	3.6	4.2	3.0	5.1	4.1
1905	3.9	4.4	3.3	5.4	
1910	4.0	4.6	3.4	5.2	4.3
1915	4.0	4.6	3.4	5.1	
1920	4.4	5.0	3.8	5.4	4.7
1930	5.5	6.0	4.9	6.5	5.4
1940	8.0	8.8	7.1	8.5	6.8
1950	9.7	10.8	8.5	10.0	8.1

SOURCES: See note 1 to this chapter.

NOTE: Percentages are rounded to nearest even place in all tables. Antebellum censuses usually excluded blacks in age tables; there were few blacks in Boston in this period.

[a] These figures are estimated by taking 60 percent of those 60 and over, the ratio found in subsequent censuses.

brought the number of people 65 and over to one-tenth of Boston's population in the 1950s.

Geographic movement of population groups helps to explain the varying rates of change. What depressed the aging rate in the nineteenth century was the migration and immigration into Boston of younger people who married and had children. What caused rapid increases in aging after 1915 were the curtailment of immigration (by World War I and

Figure II–1.
Boston Population 65 and Over as a Percentage of the Whole Population, 1830–1950

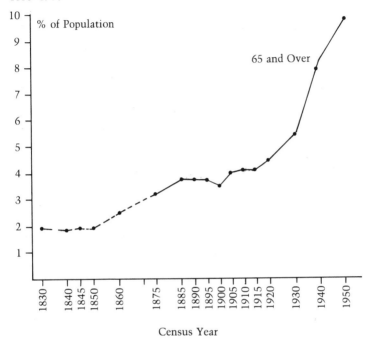

SOURCE: Table II-1.
NOTE: Broken line before 1875 is based on estimated values.

restrictive legislation), a decline in in-migration of native-born New Englanders, and an excess of out-migration from the city of young cohorts.[*][2] The youthful migrants and immigrants of the nineteenth century constituted a demo-

* A cohort is a group of persons born during a set of years, e.g., 1900–1905.

graphic timebomb; by flooding younger age brackets and by prolific reproduction characteristic of their ethnicity and age, they restrained the normal process of aging within the population; but within one or two decades, the adults reached the threshold of old age. Laws restricting immigration profoundly disturbed this demographic pattern. As soon as the stream of immigration slackened, the proportion of the elderly in the population increased far more rapidly than in a closed population. The slowing of Boston's economic growth in the twentieth century and the reduction in its attractiveness both to New Englanders in general and to its own youthful population reinforced the effects of curtailed immigration.

The varying effects of immigration can be seen first in the figures for the period 1830–1910 (Table II-1 and Figure II-1): these show an initially stable percentage of aged people during the full spate of antebellum immigration, succeeded by steady increases when war or depression intervened. In the period 1885–1915, the rate of maturation slowed as Boston experienced a second great wave of immigrants, in this instance from Italy, Russia, and Poland. After 1915, the immigration gates closed, and the city's population quickly matured.

Until well into the twentieth century, then, the Boston age structure was the mirror image of the city's structure today. Indeed, in the nineteenth century, the extraordinary concentrations of old people were found in the areas that youthful migrants and immigrants left behind. In 1895, when Boston's 60 and over cohort made up 6 percent of its population, the rural counties of Barnstable and Nantucket had 16 and 23 percent in this age stratum. Ireland's population also showed high proportions of old people, as that nation's youth emigrated.[3]

However, the perennial movement of younger people into Boston disguised regular processes of aging among particular population groups. In fact, this hidden aging helps explain two periods of concern for the aged in Boston—in 1849–1860 and 1895–1910—when the proportion of the aged actually remained stable or regressed. Native-born Bostonians and native migrants were responsible for almost all of Boston's population expansion in the 50 years before the heavy immigration of the 1840s. Between 1790 and 1840 the population of the city proper grew from 18,038 to 85,475, a consequence largely of immigration "from the depressed rural areas of New England." Substantial foreign immigration did not begin until the 1840s, and the bulk of the antebellum Irish came between 1846 and 1856.[4]

As Chapter IV describes, Boston's elite Yankees, or Brahmins, established major charities for the aged in the period 1849–1860. Since the overwhelming majority of the immigrants were relatively young, we may suppose that the overwhelming majority of Boston's aged were native-born men and women. As the Brahmins noted, many of the native elders exhibited the classic characteristics of a deprived aging population within an urban milieu. These poorer Yankee old people lived in neighborhoods rapidly filling with immigrants; they suffered the vulnerability of isolated older people in urban settings that their children have abandoned. Responding to their evident need, and revolted by the possibility that Yankee elders might mingle with the Irish in the almshouse, the Brahmins established charities to protect their ethnic brethren from the indignities of public welfare.

The second outbreak of concern for the elderly occurred in the late 1890s and early 1900s.[5] The paradox again obtains that no expansion of the proportion of the aged had occurred in Boston or in Massachusetts. A demographic explanation cannot, however, be dismissed, because there may, once more, be a disguised process of aging within a specific population group. We can explore this question by examining nativity and ethnicity among the aged population, since detailed statistics have been gathered on this point; the xenophobic temper of the turn of the century led census takers

Gender, Ethnicity, and Family

Table II–2.
Nativity and Parentage of Bostonians 65 and Over and All Ages,
1890–1950

	Persons 65 and Over			All Ages		
Census Year	Native Parents (%)	Foreign Parents[a] (%)	Foreign-Born (%)	Native Parents (%)	Foreign Parents[a] (%)	Foreign-Born (%)
1890	48.1	3.0	47.8	30.3	32.9	34.9
1900	43.3	4.6	51.0	26.1	36.9	34.8
1905	NA	NA	54.3	NA	NA	35.2
1910	38.2	7.5	53.0	23.5	38.3	36.7
1920	34.4	13.6	50.5	24.3	41.4	31.9
1930	25.5	20.6	52.1	25.6	42.2	29.4
1940[b]	25.1	20.7	51.7	35.0	38.8	23.1
1950[c]	NA	NA	52.5	NA	NA	18.1

SOURCES: See Table II-1 and see also *Sixteenth Census of the United States: 1940, Population: Nativity and Parentage of the White Population: General Characteristics* (Washington, D.C., 1943), p. 101, and *Country of Origin of the Foreign Stock* (Washington, D.C., 1943), p. 85.

NOTE: Percentages of blacks not shown. NA = not available.

[a] Having one or two foreign-born parents.

[b] 5 percent sample.

[c] 20 percent sample.

to scrutinize nativity. Table II-2 summarizes the information available on nativity and age for Boston.

Disaggregation of national to local data rewards us well here. A striking pattern manifested in Table II-2 is largely obscured in national population data. Although rarely more than one-third of the city's entire population, from 1900 to 1950 the foreign-born made up more than one-half of people 65 and over. During this period, Boston's old were predominantly *foreign*, not simply of foreign stock, but *born* in Ireland, Canada, Eastern Europe, or Southern Italy. And it is important to bear in mind that their predominance coincides with the beginning of the steady increase in the proportion of the aged within the city population as a whole.

We may safely presume that, at some point before 1890, the native-born of native parentage constituted most of Boston's aged—the earlier the date, the greater the proportion of native-born old men and women. We know that relative youth characterized most immigrants in the great antebellum waves: in 1852, 89 percent of the immigrants to the United States were less than 40 years of age and 51 percent 15 to 29.[6] If we set as the range of birthdates for this immigrant age cohort the years between 1825 and 1835, we see the source of the inevitable ascendancy of the foreign-born among the aged in the late nineteenth century. One might substitute "Irish-born" for "foreign-born," for it was the great Irish immigration into antebellum Boston that produced this elderly class. Evidence for Massachusetts indicates that in 1895, 57 percent of all foreigners 60 and over were Irish-born (the Boston percentage would be higher). The next largest foreign group, Canadians, accounted for only 12 percent. The Irish population, once abnormally youthful, had become top-heavy with the elderly: 16 percent of all Irish-born men and women were 60 and over in 1895 (about twice the level of the aged in the state population as a whole), and though the Irish made up but 10 percent of the population of the state in that year, they constituted 20 percent of the state's population 60 and over,[7] a figure certainly exceeded in Boston. In addition, nearly all the native-born aged with a foreign background would have had Irish ancestry. Certainly half of the old population in early twentieth-century Boston was Irish by birth or background.

Immigration had similar though less extreme effects nationally. Between 1890 and 1950, the foreign-born made up about one-quarter of the aged population in the United States. But in the major urban centers, the data show the same pattern found in Boston. In 1890 immigrants made up three-quarters of the aged population in New York and Chicago, and half of Philadelphia's. As late as 1950, over 60 percent of New York's elderly were foreign-born.[8]

A reasonable hypothesis connects the intensely ethnic nature of urban aging to the outbreak of concern over the aged in Massachusetts at the turn of the century.[9] Antebellum immigrants, the shock troops of the United States' first industrial offensive, had come to old age, and they tested the ability of a free enterprise economy to support its aged members. National data confirm the ethnic character of aging; from at least 1890 to 1950, the foreign-born population exceeded national averages in concentrations of the aged. In 1930, 12 percent of the foreign-born had reached 65, compared with less than 5 percent of the native population, and by 1950 the ratio was 27 percent to less than 7 percent.[10]

The Irish and other antebellum immigrants continued to fill the ranks of the aged in the early twentieth century, but by 1920 the mid-nineteenth-century foreign contribution was exhausted. Following a minor decline in the proportion of the foreign-born among the aged (1905–1920), the 1920s witnessed the renewal of the foreign influence as late nineteenth-century immigration began to assert itself in the age structure. At first the foreign-born aged remained "old immigrant stock"—that is, primarily Irish or Canadian. But as early as 1930 the impact of the new immigrants could be felt, and by 1940 natives of Italy, Russia, and Poland made up 31 percent of all foreigners aged 65 and over in Boston, a greater percentage than natives of Ireland.[11]

The political effects of the ethnic quality of aging in Boston must have been profound. During most of the twentieth century, persons of foreign birth or background made up 60 to 70 percent of the city's aged. Agitation for assistance therefore amounted to agitation for special assistance for "foreign" groups—and, initially, almost exclusively for the Irish-born. Legislation may well have been supported and opposed on just this ethnic feature. The foreign-born (and their children) would benefit most from special legislation to assist the elderly; it should therefore have been the ethnic constituencies which formed the backbone of political struggle for special assistance, and their representatives who led that struggle. As we shall see in later chapters, this was the case.

The gender characteristics of aging had bearing on the politics of age in Boston as well. Women made up 55 to 60 percent of the population 65 and over between 1875 and 1950. Since the preponderance of women in the national aged population did not generally obtain until the mid-twentieth century, the "natural" longevity of women cannot be used to explain their proportion among Boston's aged at the turn of the century. But, again, other major cities also displayed disproportionate numbers of aged women. In this period, the female majority in cities followed from immigration and migration patterns: Boston's Irish and Canadian immigrant populations featured excess numbers of females, and native-born females did not leave New England as readily as native-born men.[12] (Not only were there more aged women than men in the city, but the female population was itself "older," since the immigration of young males at the turn of the century reduced the aging of the male population.)[13]

The predominance of females in the aged population had complex effects. Since women faced woefully limited occupational opportunities, they depended essentially on men. But the old women of Boston either outnumbered or outlived them. The socially prescribed dependency of women countenanced easier access to dependency relationships in other households, particularly those of their daughters. Social welfare agencies, rigid and parsimonious as they were, tended to view the poverty of older women with greater sympathy and to provide them with assistance. Nonetheless, the position of an older woman, especially before state welfare programs were instituted, was an unenviable one, as accounts of those aided by private and public charities reveal.

The yellow newspapers' pathetic widow only slightly sensationalized a social reality of the late nineteenth and early

Table II–3.
Marital Status and Nativity of Boston Women and Men, 65 and
Over and 35–44, 1890–1950

| | 65 and Over | | | | | | 35–44 | | |
| | All | | | Foreign-Born | | | All | | |
Census Year	Sing. (%)	Md. (%)	Wd. (%)	Sing. (%)	Md. (%)	Wd. (%)	Sing. (%)	Md. (%)	Wd. (%)
Women									
1890	10.2	23.8	65.8	8.1	22.0	69.8	21.1	66.3	12.1
1900	12.2	24.5	63.0	9.6	25.5	64.6	22.1	66.7	10.4
1910	14.0	24.6	61.0	11.1	25.5	63.2	23.4	66.9	8.7
1920	16.9	24.0	58.7	12.3	25.2	62.2	23.6	67.1	8.2
1930	19.3	26.7	53.2	13.2	30.9	55.6	20.7	70.8	6.6
1940	21.7	27.0	50.6	NA	NA	NA	21.8	70.2	5.4
1950	21.0	27.3	50.8	NA	NA	NA	20.1	72.0	4.0
Men									
1890	6.6	66.0	27.2	4.9	64.7	30.3	22.5	72.9	4.1
1900	6.6	63.0	30.0	5.0	62.1	32.7	24.6	71.2	3.6
1910	8.9	59.1	31.4	6.8	59.2	33.7	23.8	72.6	3.0
1920	11.0	57.6	30.7	7.6	58.8	33.1	24.3	71.9	2.9
1930	13.2	58.4	27.4	8.4	63.4	27.5	23.8	72.5	2.4
1940	15.7	57.0	26.3	NA	NA	NA	23.5	73.2	1.7
1950	14.2	56.2	27.8	NA	NA	NA	17.8	78.3	1.2

SOURCES: *U.S. Census, 1890*, vol. 1, pt. 1, p. 888; *U.S. Census, 1900*, vol. 2, p. 312; *U.S. Census, 1910*, vol. 1, p. 617; *U.S. Census, 1920*, vol. 2, p. 468; *U.S. Census, 1930*, vol. 2, p. 952; *U.S. Census, 1940*, vol. 4, pt. 3, p. 105; *U.S. Census, 1950*. vol. 2, pt. 21, pp. 122–23.

NOTE: Blacks are excluded from data except for the 1950 census. NA = not available.

twentieth centuries, a reality that statistics on marital condition among the aged demonstrate.[14] Table II-3 presents
figures on marital condition by age and sex. The first three
columns display percentages of all females or males 65 and
over in each of three marital categories. The second three
columns show the corresponding percentages for the foreign-

born only, and the last three give percentages for comparison groups, men and women aged 35–44. In each instance these categories sum to less than 100 percent because the divorced and "unknown" have not been recorded. (The divorced were not an important category among the aged at any time during this period, and divorce had little significance even among those 35–44 until the last two census years.)

The figures underscore the difficulties of old age for women already suggested by their general predominance in the aged population. At the turn of the century, nearly two out of every three women 65 and over were widowed. To live past 64 meant that a woman was likely to live without her husband and the material as well as emotional resources he provided. In 1900 females represented 60 percent of Boston's aged population. Therefore, if one encountered 10 aged persons, 4 would be widows. Adding single females, women without a wage-earning spouse constituted nearly 5 of every 10 old persons in the city.

Across the twentieth century widowhood's share diminished; by 1950 widows made up only about half of all women over 64. However, the decline of widowhood was only secondarily a product of the increased longevity of husbands; in fact, just about the same percentage of women could expect to experience old age alone in 1950 as in 1890, since the percentage of aged single women doubled during the same period: in 1890, 24 percent of all women in the 65 and over age group had a spouse alive; in 1950 this had risen only to 27 percent.

When one compares these data with national patterns, marked differences appear. The core of potential dependency in Boston sprang from a low percentage of married women. Between 1890 and 1970, married women consistently made up about 35 percent of all females 65 and over in the United States, and single women always less than 10 percent of women of this age. Disaggregation by nativity and parentage reduces these differences somewhat, but Boston females remain decidedly more likely to be single and Boston males (again in comparison with national data) somewhat more likely to be single or widowed.[15]

But when Boston data are compared with statistics for other major cities, the deviations largely disappear. For example, in 1930 the mean percentage of married women in the aged population among cities of 500,000 or more was 30 percent, substantially lower than the national average.[16] Although Boston's proportion of single aged women remained unusually high, even compared with these other urban centers, its percentage of widows was somewhat lower. Thus, the large cities that attracted immigrants and migrants faced a similar problem: the potential or realized dependency of large segments of their aged female populations.

Foreign-born women tended toward widowed status (because fewer remained single and because of higher mortality rates among foreign-born men), especially if compared directly with native-born females. This characteristic further defined the ethnopolitical character of Boston's aged population. Before the New Deal, foreign-born widows represented 2 of every 10 older persons, and these women constituted the population most likely to experience both overt and covert dependency.

Among men many of these patterns were reversed. Generally older than their wives, and, if widowed, fortunate suitors within the surplus pool of older women, most men over 64 lived with a spouse in their old age. Differing marital statuses explain the differing social experiences of older men and women, especially at the turn of the century, when extreme marital differences by gender obtained, older women had next to no opportunity in the labor market, and few welfare programs existed. About two-thirds of all men 65 and over enjoyed the company and bore the costs of a wife. Very few failed to marry. In contradistinction to the female experience, the percentage of widowed men remained stable across time, and, as late as 1950, an older man was twice as

a nineteenth-century institution that declined in the twentieth century.[18] In fact, twentieth-century figures, especially the 1950 set, underestimate the importance of this alternative because census definitions changed.

The redefinition also distorted estimates of institutionalization. In the nineteenth century, only true inmates of institutions were so classified; the remainder (including some housed in that century's equivalent of a nursing home) were categorized as boarders and lodgers. The 1940 census classified the residents of larger boarding and lodging houses as living in "quasi households," the category for institutions as well. The 1950 census broadened the range of quasi households still further; thus, the twentieth-century censuses mixed the truly dependent with men living in bachelor contentment in large lodging houses. For 1885 and 1895, we have a much truer representation of institutionalization: the "inmates" category comprised paupers living in almshouses or boarded in families by the town's overseers of the poor, men in old age homes, prisons, and other institutions, and a few hotel residents and hospital patients. Nineteenth-century figures fairly accurately record the number of men in public and private old age institutions, whereas the twentieth-century figures exaggerate their number. In 1885 and 1895 inmates and patients amounted to 2 and 3 percent respectively of all men 60 and over. In 1940 and 1950 men in quasi households made up 6 and 9 percent of older men. (Most of the 1940 to 1950 increase in quasi-household status resulted from change in the definition of the quasi household.)[19]

If the reader will grant that the 1950 quasi-household figures especially exaggerate the number of men "institutionalized," we see that non-household living arrangements for older men increased slightly, perhaps on the order of 3 to 4 percent. The figure corresponds with the decline in the proportion of heads of households and is not a function of the deterioration of family welfare services. In a larger sense, no

Table II–6.
Marital Status of Massachusetts Men 65 and Over, 1890–1950

Census Year	Single (%)	Widowed (%)	Married (%)
1890	5.8	24.4	69.5
1920	8.4	29.8	61.2
1950[a]	10.2	26.6	62.0

SOURCE: *U.S. Census, 1950*, vol. 2, pt. 21, p. 118.

NOTE: Historical data for the marital status of men 60 and over are not uniformly available.

[a] 20 percent sample.

radical departure in social living arrangements had occurred. The proportion of older men domiciled within their own families remained remarkably stable to 1950. The great majority of older men continued to be heads of households, as they are today. Higher rates of "institutionalization," to the extent that these occurred at all, cannot be attributed to family failure. Indeed, most of the increase in nonfamilial living arrangements can be explained by a major structural change in the demography of the aged. Table II–6 reveals the pronounced expansion during the twentieth century in the percentage of single older men in Massachusetts, a phenomenon like that observed in Boston.

Common sense tells one that single men have fewer family members to rely on in old age than married men. Since the percentage of widowed men also rose, and widowers also have less access to family (the wife being the primary family resource of older men), fewer older men had families to appeal to in the mid-twentieth century than in the late nineteenth. Therefore, it should neither surprise us nor lead to criticisms of the family bond to find that a smaller proportion of older men landed in family nets. Isolated single and widowed men were more likely to be housed in boarding

Table II–7.
Household Status of Massachusetts Women, 60 and Over and
50–59, 1885–1950

	60 and Over			50–59		
Census Year	Heads (%)	Wives (%)	Mothers (%)	Heads (%)	Wives (%)	Mothers (%)
1885	28.0	34.5	22.2	20.9	58.9	5.1
1895	29.6	31.9	22.3	22.1	56.2	5.5
1940	30.9	33.5	14.2	19.2	60.3	2.9
1950	29.6	34.3	14.2	18.3	62.4	3.2

SOURCE: See Table II-4.

and lodging houses, and, as we shall see in subsequent chapters, much more vulnerable to institutionalization.[20]

The Households of Older Women

Women offer the investigator a new matrix of relationships. In 1885, in 1895, and also in 1940 and 1950, about 30 percent of all Massachusetts women 60 and over headed households—there was no change in more than half a century (Table II-7). These levels, substantially lower than men's, nonetheless exceeded the rates for younger women (for example, in 1885 only 5 percent and, in 1950, 6 percent of women aged 30–39 headed households). Although becoming head of the household was one consequence of widowhood (and often a bitter inheritance), this role was not common among older women. The most characteristic family status remained that of the wife of the household head. Again no change occurred between the nineteenth and twentieth centuries: about one-third of older women reported themselves as wives of heads of households.

Comparison with the 50–59 age group shows, however, that the fraction of wives was sharply reduced among older women. In each of the censuses, the 50 percent drop in the wives category between the 50–59 and the 60 and over group (the result of increased widowhood) created dramatic shifts within the family support system. The nature of these shifts changed radically between the nineteenth and twentieth centuries.

First, Table II-7 makes it plain that in both centuries a very large proportion of women who experienced old age did so in the homes of children. Between two and three times as many women as men resided as a dependent parent in both historical periods. Some scholars explain this difference as a function of the readier acceptance of the submissive female in the household of the dominant male, but the sheer numbers of widowed women (at any of these censuses they outnumbered widowers by two or three to one) and the ability of older men to support themselves through work offer more satisfactory explanations.

In the nineteenth century, however, a much larger part of the aged female population lived in their children's homes; more than one-fifth of all Massachusetts women 60 and over resided (presumably as subordinates) in the homes of children in the late nineteenth century. Since only about 14 percent lived in such homes in the twentieth century, the figures appear to confirm for women the charge that the family abandoned its function of providing for the aged—a charge found to be without substance for aged males in Massachusetts up to 1950. Recalling that analysis of men, we must include among women supported by the family those who are aunts, cousins, and so on. Table II-8 provides the percentages of women 60 and over related to the head of the household but not wives or heads themselves; the last column displays the percentage of all older women living in familial households, including wives and female heads of households. (Some women counted as "heads" may actually be living alone.)

The slight increase in the twentieth century in the pro-

Table II–8.
Massachusetts Women 60 and Over Related to the Head and in
All Family Relationships, 1885–1950

Census Year	Related to Head (Not Spouses) (%)	Total "In Family" (Heads, Spouses, Related) (%)
1885	29.1	91.6
1895	29.6	91.1
1940	22.8	87.2
1950	22.6	86.5

SOURCE: See Table II-4.

portion of women housed by relatives other than their sons or daughters somewhat counteracted declines in the percentages living with sons and daughters. When we consider all women who live in family environments—as relatives, wives, or heads of households—we see that the perception that families have become derelict in their duty is of limited usefulness in understanding the experience of older women. The decline in the percentage provided households by their children is important, but slightly greater proportions of twentieth-century women cared for themselves, lived with their husbands, or resided with other relatives. (It is worth noting that aged men and women enjoyed family living arrangements in about the same percentages.) The true decline in the percentage living within the family environment amounted to 4 to 5 percent.

One might argue, as a Dorchester woman did, that a greater decline in family "security" occurred than is apparent because servants who "lived in" enjoyed the benefits of family life.[21] Domestic service was more common among women than men. Women living as servants in another family's household accounted for a small percentage of women 60 and over: in 1885, 1.8 percent, 1895, 2.0 percent, 1940,

Table II–9.
Massachusetts Women 60 and Over Boarding and Lodging, in All
Households, and Living as Inmates or in Quasi Households,
1885–1950

Census Year	Boarding and Lodging (%)	All Households[a] (%)	Inmates/Quasi Households (%)
1885	4.3	97.7	1.9
1895	4.3	97.4	2.4
1940	6.1	95.0	4.9
1950	4.4	92.1	7.9

SOURCE: See Table II-4.

[a] Includes family households, boarding and lodging, and service.

1.7 percent, and 1950, 1.2 percent. Estimating an average
decline of 0.5 percent in this arrangement makes the general
decline of women living in "family" households equal to
about 5 percent.

Although we must bear in mind the problems of definition
and consistency that attend data on boarding, lodging, and
institutionalization, Table II-9 provides census statistics for
boarding and lodging, a total for all older women living in
family and nonfamily households, and the percentages listed
as "inmates" in the nineteenth century and as residents of
quasi households in the twentieth.

Boarding and lodging persisted as an alternative form of
living for older women. Comparisons between censuses are
confounded by the changing definition of boarding and lodging in the 1940 and 1950 censuses. As noted in the analysis
for men, these censuses placed some residents of boarding
and lodging houses in quasi households, mixing them with
truly institutionalized persons. The 1950 census in particular inflates the quasi-household category. On the conservative assumption that one-third of the 1940–1950 increase
is due to the change in categorization, an adjusted figure for

Table II–10.
Marital Status of Massachusetts Women 65 and Over, 1890–1950

Census Year	Single (%)	Widowed (%)	Married (%)
1890	8.7	59.6	31.5
1920	13.1	58.0	28.5
1950[a]	16.6	50.3	32.3

SOURCE: *U.S. Census, 1950*, vol. 2, pt. 21, p. 118.

NOTE: Historical data for the marital status of women 60 and over are not uniformly available.

[a] 20 percent sample.

1950 would equal 7 percent. The average increase from the nineteenth to the twentieth century in those not living in households (with some boarders and lodgers still misplaced) thus amounts to about 4 percent.

Once again, the family cannot be charged with dereliction of its duty. A new class of older women arose by the mid-twentieth century in Massachusetts, one more likely than other groups to board and lodge (hence, more likely to be placed in the quasi-household category) and much more likely actually to be institutionalized in old age; a corresponding diminution occurred in that class most likely to have a family to rely on and live with, thus avoiding these alternative living situations. Table II–10 demonstrates the momentous shift of a large part of the population of older women from widowed to single status in the period 1890–1950. Although the widow faced true perils, her chances of having surviving children to rely on stood rather higher than those of her single peer. Indeed, the larger percentage of mothers living in the households of their sons and daughters in the nineteenth century directly reflected the demographic condition that more widowed mothers were available to more children, a circumstance whose implications subsequent analysis in this chapter will make clear. The single woman had the least chance among older women of having a family to rely on and, according to contemporary social gerontology, the highest probability of being institutionalized.[22] Naturally, she (and the single man) would be more likely than others to resort to alternatives to the family living environment in boarding and lodging houses, and, if truly dependent, to enter an institution.

Filial Duty and the Aging Parent

In investigating the living circumstances of older people in Massachusetts between 1885 and 1950, we have found a decrease in family living from about 91 percent to about 87 percent. The 4 percent decline includes some aged who boarded and lodged and others who lived in institutions; it has been difficult to separate the two. Even if we succeeded in distinguishing between them, the differences would be in part artificial because by the mid-twentieth century "boarding houses were being transformed into 'homes for the aged,'" causing a "large part" of the shift in categories.[23] In the nineteenth century, unlicensed and privately financed boarding houses fulfilled a function equivalent to that of the nursing home. On the whole the most impressive data underscore the continuity of the family in the household arrangements of the aged. When we consider the increase in the proportion of the aged in the population (and, thus, the decline in the relative size of the younger, supporting generation) and the increase in the proportion of single old persons, the slight decline in family living seems reasonably well explained by structural and demographic changes, and no recourse is needed to the effects of changes in attitudes or in the norms of family life.

We can subject this argument to further test, combining the analyses of men and women. Up to this point, investigation has focused on the relationship of the older person to

Table II–11.
Male and Female Age Groups in Households as "Children,"
Massachusetts, 1885–1950

	Age Group								Summary Group	
	20–29		30–39		40–49		50–59		30–59	
Census	M (%)	F (%)	M (%)	F (%)	M (%)	F (%)	M (%)	F (%)	M (%)	F (%)
1885	38	33	10	12	3	5	1	2	5.6	7.5
1895	37	33	10	13	4	6	1	2	6.0	7.9
1940	58	46	16	16	5	7	1	2	8.1	9.1
1950	41	34	12	14	5	7	2	3	6.7	8.2

SOURCE: See Table II-4.

the household: head, spouse, father of the head, and so on. In the classic case of intrafamilial support, however, a grown son or daughter, usually single, stays at home with aging parents. Scholars have argued that one great difference between the lots of the nineteenth-century and twentieth-century aged is that the spinster daughter no longer agrees to remain in the household as helpmate of the old folks.[24]

This interpretation, already suspect for Massachusetts because so many older people never married and hence had no children, can be examined directly in the census tables dealing with household relationships. Using data for adult men and women whose status remained that of son or daughter of the head (including step-, adopted, and grandchildren), we construct a measure of filial responsibility in the support of aged parents.

Contrary to expectation, at every age group between 19 and 60, the percentage of men and women remaining in their parents' households in the twentieth century exceeds nineteenth-century levels (Table II-11). That is, an adult child,

35 years of age, in Massachusetts in 1950 was *more* likely to live with his aging parents than his peer in 1885. In *no* instance does a nineteenth-century figure exceed its twentieth-century counterpart. If those 20–29 are deleted as possibly still of dependent age, the age group 30–59 provides a summary indicator of family living arrangements of this type. The summary measures in Table II-11 show clearly the unexpected trend across time. In the twentieth century it was more likely that an adult son or daughter would remain in the household of his or her parents.

What then is the source of the myth of callous modern youth? For Massachusetts it was simply this: the size of the aged population increased much more rapidly than the size of the population of children who might support them. We may compare the census periods directly, dividing the absolute number of those adults still reporting their household status as "children" by the absolute number of those 60 and over. This gives us a direct measure of the capacity of the family-support mechanism. In the nineteenth century, the ratios of children aged 30–59 to the population 60 and over averaged 0.28; in the twentieth, 0.23. Although a larger percentage of all adults stayed at home with aged parents, they still could not "serve" as many of the elderly. In Massachusetts the rising proportion of old people strained the capacity of their children to maintain household support. In other words, and assuming motive, we have found that the children tried even harder to do their duty; a larger proportion stayed home, but they could not keep pace with the aging of the population.

To the contemporary observer, what makes the continuity to 1950 most striking is the dramatic *discontinuity* since that date. After 1950 the household status of the elderly underwent radical change. Now very large percentages of old people, especially women, live alone, in isolation from other family members. Given the stability of the family welfare tradition observed across the period 1885–1950, this contemporary isolation appears remarkable. Why has the disintegration of the family household occurred?

Conclusions:
Households in the
Welfare State

Analysis of census data for Boston and Massachusetts has revealed the salience of immigration in the historical demography of old age. This in turn implies the force of ethnic concerns in old age politics. Families, the welfare institution of the pre–social security era, tended to bear the burden of supporting older people. Because, as investigation of Boston's occupational conditions will demonstrate, most older men remained in the labor force during this period and thus retained household independence, old women constituted the essence of the "welfare problem."

Between 1885–95 and 1940–50, the evidence on household arrangements suggests that the effort of the family unit to sustain its aged members changed very little, confirming Daniel Scott Smith's argument that the family changes at a glacial pace. By a reasonable measure of the adult children's willingness to remain with their aged parents, the cohorts of the mid-twentieth century showed themselves to be as dutiful as their nineteenth-century counterparts. In the first half of the twentieth century, little change in household arrangements occurred, and the changes that did can be attributed to compositional changes in the aged population.[25]

In the postwar period, however, dramatic shifts can be observed. The household arrangements of persons 60 and over in Massachusetts in 1980 are displayed in Table II-12. The statistics indicate that, among males, headship (now called "householder") has increased since the 1950s (75 to 86 percent) and is, indeed, greater than in nineteenth-century censuses. The proportion living with relatives has fallen only slightly from earlier periods (from 10–11 to 9 percent).

Table II–12.
Household Status of Massachusetts Men and Women, 60 and
Over, 1980

	Males (%)	Females (%)
Householders	85.5	45.1
(Family)	(72.0)	(11.3)
(Living Alone)	(12.8)	(32.8)
Spouses	3.7	35.8
Parents	1.7	4.4
Otherwise Related	3.6	6.7
Non-Related	1.1	1.0
Group Quarters	4.4	7.0
Total	100.0	100.0

SOURCES: U.S. Department of Commerce, Bureau of the Census, *1980 Census of Population*, vol. 1, *Characteristics of the Population*, Chapter D, *Detailed Population Statistics*, pt. 23, *Massachusetts*, pp. 83, 86, 107.

Generally speaking, between 1950 and 1980 little or no decline occurred in family household living for older men.

Older women tell another tale. The percentage of women who are householders has increased radically (from about 30 percent to 45 percent), and three quarters of these women live alone. While the proportion who live as spouses has stayed remarkably constant since the nineteenth century, the proportion otherwise related to the head has declined precipitously since 1950. The impetus in this decline has been change in older women's coresidence with their children. In 1950, 14 percent of women 60 and over lived as a parent to the household head. In 1980, 4.4 percent did. The substitution appears manifest: older women now live alone rather than with children.

As many scholars have noted, the share of the aged population enjoying married life has remained about the same throughout the twentieth century. But the proportion living with relatives has sharply declined, and the proportion living alone or with nonrelatives has just as precipitously increased. For example, Daniel Scott Smith shows that in 1900, 29 percent of those 65 and over resided with relatives and only 6 percent lived alone or outside the family; in 1980 inverse conditions obtained: 9 percent lived with relatives, and 29 percent lived alone or outside the family.[26] In particular, the proportion living with married children has declined. These isolated "primary individuals," largely widowed women, once almost invariably lived in their daughters' homes.

After adjustment for changes in the composition of the aged population (such as proportion married), the net shift in the twentieth century toward living alone appears to be entirely a product of the postwar era. The debate among scholars attempting to explain the great shift toward isolation revolves around the issue of economic or normative causation. Partisans of the former explanation argue that a "threshold income," reached after World War II, created the opportunity for different generations to enjoy separate living arrangements. Empirical research supports the argument that income determines living arrangements, since in recent cross-sectional studies poorer families were more likely than wealthier ones to house an aging parent. A common variant of the income approach views the welfare state's social security benefits as providing the aged with the means to set up separate households. According to this school, the norm of separate living dominated at all times, but could not be realized until recently. Historical research documenting the durability and persistence of the northwestern European family pattern of separate nuclear households supports this interpretation.[27]

Nonetheless, some scholars argue that a decline in the normative value of intrafamilial coresidence and support constitutes the true cause of the shift toward separate living. Thus, *all* age groups have tended to set up separate households in recent times, and at rates faster than income ad-

vances would predict. Many older Americans complain that
the family once took care of its own, but these values have
since been abandoned. Daniel Scott Smith has produced historical evidence to buttress the normative explanation, aim-
ing, quite correctly, at the threshold income concept as the
principal competing explanation. Using cross-sectional data
from a sample of the 1900 manuscript census schedules, he
argues that income differences at the turn of the century did
not predict living arrangements. In the most persuasive evidence, older people from middle-class environments were
found to be more likely than the working-class aged to live
with adult children. Thus, in contrast to current conditions,
families with greater relative incomes tended to extend their
households to the aged more often than poorer families.[28]

However, a fundamental error is committed here. *Real*
income, not relative income, affects the choices of families
faced with housing and caring for old relatives. Let us examine the real income of individuals and families in 1900:
that is, their actual capacity to obtain housing, food, domestic assistance, and so on. The annual per capita gross
national product in 1970 was $4,808. Adjusted for inflation,
per capita gross national product in 1900 was about $1,370;
disposable real income per capita increased from about
$1,000 per year in 1900 to $3,400 per year in 1970. Stanley
Lebergott estimates that nonfarm families had an average
income in 1900 (adjusted to 1970 dollars) of about $5,100.
Lebergott's estimates of the distribution of income in 1900,
again adjusted to 1970 dollars, are as follows for nonfarm
families:

> 75 percent: less than $5,100;
> 21 percent: from $5,100 to $7,300;
> 4 percent: greater than $7,300.

If we assume that these three categories reflect working-
class, middle-class, and upper-class incomes in 1900 (a conservative estimate of the size of the middle class), the pov-

erty of the turn-of-the-century middle class is obvious. In 1970, 80 percent of families in the United States had incomes greater than $5,000 per year, 27 percent had incomes between $10,000 and $14,999, and 22 percent enjoyed incomes in excess of $14,999. Among "unrelated individuals," a category in which the newly isolated aged figure heavily, 44 percent had incomes greater than $5,000. It is reasonable to conclude that many of the isolated elderly command resources which exceed those of entire families in the middle class in 1900. These incomes permit such individuals to live alone.[29]

Given their larger families, the income available to the middle class in 1900 hardly seems conducive to the provision of separate living quarters for aged members. Indeed, their income approximates that of just those groups in contemporary society most likely to have to extend their households. The threshold income thesis demands real income estimates, since these tell us what choices families could make about housing arrangements. In 1900 only a minuscule proportion of the population had the range of alternatives that a great majority have today.

In view of the relative poverty of the early twentieth-century family, an income argument—and, more specifically, one based on the rise of welfare provisions for the aged—offers a more plausible explanation of changes in household type. Using national data, Alvin Schorr demonstrated that the 1950s trend toward separate living was accelerated among the aged receiving Social Security insurance benefits.[30] As the historical and contemporary data indicate, aged women compose the chief population-at-risk in all periods. In the early twentieth century, most aged males remained in the labor force. By the middle of the century, males' work-related social security income had replaced job income; in effect, aged men maintained an income-based independence, and their household position did not markedly change. Women, however, did not generally have work-related income; usually they relied on their families for income, primarily as wives of the wage-earning household heads. In old age, widows and even single women had to turn to relatives other than spouses for income assistance. Once the most likely to dwell with a daughter or daughter-in-law,[31] such women now live alone. As the next chapter will demonstrate, widows in particular had in the past little choice but to move in with a child, since the labor market offered them only the worst jobs. But with Old Age Assistance, and especially after amendment of the Social Security Act in 1939 and subsequent liberalization, public welfare did not demand of women an income history;[32] they could collect benefits on the basis of their husbands' previous income.

Francis Kobrin shows for national population groups what was found for Massachusetts cohorts: across the twentieth century, the ratio of aged "parents" to adult "children" increased dramatically and became, he argues, too great to be sustained by the norm of intrafamilial support.[33] Smith rejects Kobrin's argument, showing that in 1900 a woman with only one child was nearly as likely to live with a child as a woman with five children (79 percent versus 89 percent). For Smith this finding indicates that declines in coresidence after World War II were "primarily due to changes in the propensity to form these types of households," not to a declining number of available children.[34] As Smith remarks, given the associated probabilities, "one child was nearly as good as five."[35]

For the old woman perhaps, but hardly for the children. From their point of view, the probabilities mean something else: with four siblings, an adult child had a relatively low chance of being called upon to share the household with the aging mother. Across the twentieth century, in the United States as well as Massachusetts, the possibility of escaping the burden of support shrank drastically. Larger fractions of adults remained in parental households in Massachusetts in 1950 than in 1885. More and more adult children faced the difficult choices always present when an aged parent approaches dependency. The reason that the number of children made so little difference in 1900 was that the demand was inelastic: no matter how few children, the family had to support one old mother. Across the century, as birth rates declined, the choice fell more and more often upon married children, already out of the house and independent. These children violated the norm of autonomous nuclear family units by extending the household to the aged.[36]

Kobrin believes that the norms of intrafamilial support were too weak to meet this challenge and that postwar society witnessed a "major redefinition of the appropriate family group": "Under pressure from demographic changes, then, residence norms have changed, resulting in a great increase in the proportion of older females who live alone."[37] It appears more likely that the true norm had always been separate living quarters, or, if you will, that such households presented the optimal arrangement. Nonetheless, families loathed the almshouse and the old age home; they would open up their households to protect the aged from these indignities. Although it is unlikely that either generation wanted coresidence, neither had an income level that permitted separate maintenance of the elderly. The same old Bostonians of the 1970s who fondly recalled the time when the family took care of its aged wanted now to live separate and independent lives. When describing the past, these old people without exception shared a nostalgic and sometimes accurate impression that "nobody ever thought of not taking care of their own." Some resentment of the present appears in this recollection. But just beneath its surface lie memories of discord in the household, of the economic, as opposed to affective, motives for sharing a home: one mother "shed a good many tears over . . . old Gram's attitude," and another, cracking under the strain of her duties, blurted out to a bedridden grandmother, "I don't know what we'll do if you live another year."[38]

The demand for coresidence in 1900 was slight: by one researcher's measure, only one in three adult daughters was likely to be tested on it. In 1980, *sans* social security, almost every female adult would have to exhibit allegiance to filial duty. The pressure built steadily across the century: as the aged increased in proportion within the population, they brought more and more weight to bear on the family to provide support.[39] In Boston, ethnic subpopulations periodically endured periods in which they contained a large part of the city's aged population. The dependents among this older group were generally women. Men maintained independence through work and, after the New Deal, through the Social Security benefits gained from work. Widowed women, as the next chapter will demonstrate, had great difficulty in supporting themselves through work. The rise of the welfare state, then, had very important implications for aged women. Subject to supporting the aging mother, ethnic, working-class populations in Boston had good reason to seek relief outside the family. It was the New Deal, and the continued expansion of Social Security benefits for women whether they worked outside the home or not, that made the ideal of separate and independent households attainable for many American families.

Chapter III
The Veterans
of Labor

Nothing is more critical to an understanding of the place of the elderly in American society than analysis of their labor force activity over time. These are depths often sounded but still ill-charted. Chapter I explored the continuing controversy over whether, when, and why old people lost occupational position. Most scholars view declines in the labor force participation of older males as constant and rapid from the late nineteenth century to the present. Modernization theorists state that this precipitous withdrawal from work has resulted from urban-industrial conditions, which made older workers less valuable. Attitudinalists argue that ageism—a negative cultural view of older people—led employers to believe that older workers were less efficient than younger ones. Each of these views suggests that the demand for older workers steadily declined from the late nineteenth century to the present.

This chapter argues on the contrary that no precipitate decline occurred in the early twentieth century. Rather, in advanced sectors like Boston, the percentage of older men who stayed in the labor force remained stable between 1890 and 1930. Although their labor force activity was not as great as that of younger men, most older men worked during this time. Among older women, labor force participation rates actually increased in the early twentieth century. After 1930, however, sharp declines occurred for men, the most probable cause being the availability of welfare benefits upon which to retire. Thus, the *supply* of older workers declined when alternative forms of income became available to them.

The second principal argument drawn from the Boston data questions the level of ageism operating in the labor market. The use of a cohort approach to examine specific occupations in Boston reveals some clearly discriminatory practices, but the more general pattern is one in which newer occupations, initially dominated by the young, "age" and eventually include many older workers. Compared with all age groups, Boston's aged had unequal access to some occupations at any given point, but access changed over time: job categories once staffed overwhelmingly by young people underwent a process of aging and showed increasing fractions of older workers in later census years. The tendency to interpret age-specific occupational distribution at a single time as a sign of long-term decline for aged workers obscures the occupational history of the elderly because it ignores cohort effect, the characteristics, independent of age, that are particular to people born in the same period. (For instance, education tends to differ by cohort.)

The relatively low participation rates and disproportionate occupational distribution of older workers, well established in Boston by 1890, probably reflected the fundamental effects on the aged of the transition from an agrarian economy to a commercial and industrial one. In fact, one reading of Boston's occupational data is that rapid change in occupational requirements always threatens older workers. There has been little historical study of the older worker that addresses these questions. Statistics for analysis over time—that is, census data—are fraught with inconsistencies and methodological stumbling blocks. These problems are rendered somewhat less acute by focusing on a single city, where relative uniformity of occupational structure prevailed (unlike larger units, which mix industrial and agrarian labor forces). Although reliable data before 1890 are difficult to find, in that year the census began consistently to provide labor force information on men and women 65 and over.

The following analysis of census data from 1890 to 1950 utilizes two conventional measures. The labor force participation *rate* (LFPR) simply measures the percentage of the elderly population who state that they are workers—that is, not retired; the labor force or occupational *percentage* measures what part older workers make up of the labor force or of a specific occupation. Although various inconsistencies limit comparisons across census years, the principal change in labor force measurement came in 1940, when the census stipulated that only persons employed or *actively* seeking work should be considered to be in the labor force. Since the pre-1940 "gainful worker" definition probably included many older men who were not actively seeking work, I have used adjustment ratios developed by John D. Durand for the pre-1940 censuses.[1]

Older Workers and the New Deal

Male Workers
in Boston

Table III-1 records the unexpected course of labor force participation among older Boston men: in the 40-year period from 1890 to 1930, no dramatic decline occurred (59 to 55 percent, adjusted rates); the steep drop followed in the single decade of the depression and the New Deal, when the rate fell to 35 percent; and it stood in the relatively prosperous year of 1950 at less than 40 percent. Older men participated in the pre–New Deal labor force at two-thirds the rate of younger men, but these conditions, established by 1890,[2] did not change much in what some scholars have

Table III–1.
Labor Force Activity of Men 65 and Over, Boston, 1890–1950: Percentage of Male Population, Percentage of Male Labor Force, and LFPR

Census Year	Males 65 and Over			Labor Force		LFPR		
	As % of Male Population	As % of Males 10 and Over	As % of Males 14 and Over	% 65 and Over		65 and Over		Other Ages
				Adjusted	Unadjusted	Adjusted	Unadjusted	Unadjusted
1890	3.3	4.0		2.9	3.1	59.4	64.2	25–44: 96.4
1900	3.0	3.7		2.8	3.0	59.7	64.6	45–64: 92.5
1910	3.4	4.2		NA	NA	NA	NA	NA
1920	3.8	4.7		3.4	3.6	57.9	62.6	45–64: 95.4
1930	4.9	5.9		4.3	4.5	54.6	59.0	35–44: 97.3
1940	7.1		8.9	4.0[a]	4.0[a]	34.6	34.6	35–44: 93.4
1950[b]	8.5		10.9	5.7[a]	5.7[a]	38.4	38.4	35–44: 92.6

SOURCES: U.S. Department of the Interior, Census Office, *Report on Population of the United States at the Eleventh Census: 1890*, vol. 1, pt. 2 (Washington, D.C., 1897), pp. 116, 638–39; [U.S. Department of Commerce and Labor], Census Office, Census Office, Census Reports, vol. 2: *Twelfth Census of the United States Taken in the Year 1900, Population*, pt. 2 [vol. 2] (Washington, D.C., 1902), p. 124, and *Special Reports . . . Occupations* (Washington, D.C., 1904), p. 498; U.S. Department of Commerce, Bureau of the Census, *Thirteenth Census of the United States Taken in the Year 1910*, vol. 1: *Population: 1910*, (Washington, D.C., 1913), p. 438; *Fourteenth Census of the United States Taken in the Year 1920*, vol. 2, *Population, 1920: General Report and Analytical Tables* (Washington, D.C., 1922), p. 289, and vol. 4, *Population. 1920: Occupations* (Washington, D.C., 1923), pp. 452–55, 1062–64; *Fifteenth Census of the United States: 1930, Population*, vol. 3, *Reports by States*, pt. 1 (Washington, D.C., 1932), pp. 1083, 1091, and vol. 4, *Occupations*, (Washington, D.C., 1933), pp. 728, 730, 755; *Sixteenth Census of the United States: 1940, Population*, vol. 2, *Characteristics of the Population*, pt. 3 (Washington, D.C., 1943) p. 670, and vol. 3, *The Labor Force*, pt. 3. (Washington, D.C., 1943), pp. 453, 457, 562–65, and vol. 4, *Characteristics by Age*, pt. 3 (Washington, D.C., 1943), p. 175; *Census of Population: 1950*, vol. 2: *Characteristics of the Population*, pt. 21: *Massachusetts* (Washington, D.C., 1952), pp. 58, 113, 152, 155, 208–10. Also see the display of population figures in chapter II. Subsequent citations will be in short form.

NOTE: Adjusted figures are based on the adjustment ratios given in John D. Durand, *The Labor Force in the United States, 1890–1960* (New York, 1948), p. 199.

ᵃ In 1940 men 65 and over made up 4.4 percent of all employed men not working on public emergency projects. In 1950 men 65 and over were 5.9 percent of all such employed men.

ᵇ Labor Force and LFPR figures based on a 20 percent sample.

Table III–2.
Labor Force Activity of Men 65 and Over, United States, 1890–
1950: Percentage of Male Labor Force and LFPR

Census Year	Adjusted		Unadjusted	
	% of Labor Force	LFPR	% of Labor Force	LFPR
1890	4.6	68.3	4.7	73.8
1900	4.3	63.1	4.5	68.4
1920	4.3	55.6	4.4	60.1
1930	4.8	53.9	5.1	58.3
1940	4.6	42.2	4.6	42.2
1950	5.5	41.5	5.5	41.5

SOURCES: Durand, *Labor Force*, pp. 196, 208; Gertrude Bancroft, *The American Labor Force* (New York, 1958), pp. 202, 207; Alba M. Edwards, *Sixteenth Census of the United States: Population: Comparative Occupation Statistics for the United States, 1870 to 1940,* (Washington, D.C., 1943), pp. 93, 95.

characterized as the critical period in the history of the aged worker. The Boston data for 1890–1930 raise serious questions about conventional accounts of the plight of the aged worker before the Social Security Act. But the data for 1930–1950 also pose difficulties for the view that Social Security saved older men whose long-term decline in labor force activity proved their inability to compete in the labor market. Indeed, the stability of labor force participation before 1930, its collapse after that date, and its continued decline to the present suggest that public welfare was less a response to the difficulties of older workers in the labor market than an instrument in their removal from it.

The participation rates of older workers in the nation as a whole offer an interesting comparison. Unadjusted and adjusted figures (using the Durand ratios), presented in Table III-2, show a much steeper decline than Boston experienced to 1920, a slight fall across the next decade, and renewed decline after 1930. National participation rates began well above Boston's in 1890 (68 percent versus 59 percent) but by 1930 had settled at the same general level (54 percent versus 55 percent).

Continued declines after 1930 misled scholars, who describe twentieth-century decreases in LFPR as "pronounced and continuous during the whole period."[3] In fact, before the 1930s, LFPRs were moving toward a relatively stable level. As the United States shifted away from an agriculturally based economy (where participation rates of older men are incontestably higher than in urban, industrial economies) and toward the urbanized society already well established in Boston in 1890, LFPR showed first a rapid decline and then stabilization at a level similar to Boston's relatively constant one. The mean annual rate of decline between 1890 and 1930 was 0.36 percent; the annual rate between 1930 and 1950 was 0.62 percent, almost twice as rapid.

This shift can be demonstrated using data generated by W. Andrew Achenbaum to prove quite the opposite point— that is, that national LFPR among older men began to decline precipitously at the end of the nineteenth century and continued to collapse across the twentieth. From this point of view, social security appears to have been a rescue mission for older workers unable to hold on to their jobs. According to Achenbaum, negative "perceptions" of the aged started to affect their LFPR at the turn of the century. To support this contention he reviewed various occupational and labor force statistics from 1890 to 1970. Table III-3 reproduces Achenbaum's essential data, which consist of "drop-off ratios" for each census year for agricultural occupations (including fishing and mining), nonagricultural occupations, and "all" occupations. The drop-off ratio compares the proportion of the male population 65 and over engaged in an occupational category with the proportion of the 45–64-year-old male population working in that category. Thus, in 1900 the proportion of aged males in agriculture was 93 percent of the proportion of men 45–64 so engaged. For nona-

The Veterans of Labor

Table III-3.
Rate of Drop-Off of Males from the Labor Force with Advancing Age, 1890–1970

Census Year	Agriculture (%)	Nonagricultural Occupations (%)	All Occupations (%)
1890	89	58	77
1900	93	59	74
1920	82	53	64
1930	90	52	62
1940	87	44	55
1950	84	38	46
1960	68	30	34
1970	56	26	28

SOURCE: W. Andrew Achenbaum, *Old Age in the New Land* (Baltimore, 1978), p. 103, table 5.6, based on census data; the author does not indicate whether figures were adjusted for changes from "gainful worker" to "labor force" concepts.

NOTE: The drop-off ratio is established by dividing the proportion of males 65 and over engaged in an occupational category by the proportion of males 45–64 engaged in that occupational category and multiplying the result by 100 percent.

gricultural occupations the figure is 59 percent, and for the combined categories, 74 percent. The ratio provides one measure of the falling participation of older workers in comparison with other workers.[4] Examining this evidence, Achenbaum argues that

> data in [Table III-3] reveal that the ratio of men over sixty-five years old in all occupations was 77% as large as that of men working between the ages of forty-five and sixty-four in 1890. It dropped fifteen percentage points over the next forty years and has plummeted thirty-four additional points during the past forty years. Significantly, this long-term trend exists in both the agricultural and nonagrarian sectors of the economy.[5]

Long-term trends are revealed here, but they are not what Achenbaum makes of them.

Let us examine the period 1890–1930 in particular. Achenbaum notes without comment that the 40 years after 1930 showed more dramatic losses, but his attention to a 15-percentage-point drop in the previous 40-year period obscures its cause. In agricultural occupations there was *no* drop-off in the entire period from 1890 to 1930; there were only variations. Older men maintained their position relative to men 45 to 64. In nonagricultural occupations older men showed a 6 percent decline across 40 years. (Note that the ratio of older men to younger men was always low in nonagricultural pursuits, rendering doubtful Achenbaum's optimism about the status of the aged industrial worker before 1890.)

Turning to "all occupations," the combination of the stable agricultural area and the slightly declining nonagricultural one, we find a 15 percent decline between 1890 and 1930. Since neither of the component categories fell abruptly, what explains the decline in all occupations? The explanation lies in the relationship between component categories, for what happened was that the labor force moved from the advantageous-to-the-aged agricultural area to the lower-participation nonagricultural area. It is this movement—part of the transition from an agricultural to an industrial society—that explains the overall drop, not a change in participation rates themselves. This finding suggests that shifts in attitudes, which should have affected both component and combined categories, are less important than long-term structural change in the economy.

The calamitous effects of the 1930s and 1940s—depression and New Deal years—radically transformed this pattern of stable component rates and gradual overall decline. Quite suddenly the drop-off ratio in nonagricultural occupations fell precipitously, and after 1950 (when certain Social Security programs were extended to farm work), the ratio dropped in agriculture as well. All occupations followed suit: a trump card for the aged worker. All categories and combinations reflect the hasty departure of the aged from the post-1930 labor force. It is quite clear that we have viewed two distinct patterns in the work experience of the aged and two different periods in their history.

Further evidence for the structural shift can be found by examining other urban areas. The relatively slight decline in Boston between 1890 and 1930, followed by sharp losses after 1930, outlines the general urban pattern. In 1890 aged men in the 50 largest American cities had a mean adjusted LFPR of 61 percent. This fell 8 points, to 53 percent, across the next 40 years. But between 1930 and 1950, labor force participation declined 12 percentage points to 41 percent. The annual rate of decline trebled after 1930. On the whole, the larger and more developed the city, the less rapid the declines in labor force participation before 1930. After 1930, urban, nonurban, industrial, and agrarian sectors converged to the same low participation rate.[6]

Initially, low participation rates in advanced urban areas followed from a variety of causes, including the greater wealth available for retirement[7] and the deleterious impact of wage employment on some older workers. But in such places labor force activity did not continue to decline rapidly but rather stabilized with more than half of all older men remaining in the labor force. After 1930 the shape of the curve depicting participation in urban areas changed radically, sloping down very rapidly. Whether older men had previously worked out of desire or necessity remains unclear, but by 1950, in both urban and rural areas, they were much less likely to work at all.

The dramatic acceleration of retirement after 1930 stems directly from the rise of the welfare state. As subsequent analysis of Boston's occupational conditions will indicate, certain segments of the aged labor force were especially susceptible to chronic unemployment, and the depression exacerbated their difficulties. By the relatively crude measures of the 1930s, older men had higher rates of unemployment than younger men. However, the differences in unemployment are not sufficient to explain the collapse in labor force participation by the elderly during the 1930s, and data from the same period show that a large part of the aged labor force was *more* secure in employment than younger workers.[8] Many older workers were privileged employees, valued by their employers and the last to be laid off. It seems incontestable that the provision of public old age benefits induced many older workers to retire, drawing out the more marginal ones first, but also offering the better-established worker an alternative to the job. In 1950, when unemployment was not a striking problem, fewer than four in every ten men 65 and over worked.

Although economists have gathered an impressive body of evidence showing that the old age insurance provisions of the Social Security Act have reduced LFPR among older men, they confine their argument to the period since 1950, when such Social Security benefits became more generous and covered nearly all workers.[9] But the welfare state actually began in Boston in the 1920s and expanded rapidly. In 1931 Massachusetts put into effect an old age assistance act (OAA), a relief measure commonly viewed as an older worker's pension. Massachusetts OAA, enriched by federal monies in 1936 through the Social Security Act, was an extremely far-reaching and generous program. During the 1940s, Social Security insurance augmented the direct assistance programs, providing a higher real monthly pension in the early 1940s than in 1950.[10]

As William Graebner has argued, the architects of social security policy in the Roosevelt administration saw old age benefits as a way to reduce unemployment by drawing older workers out of the labor force. In addition, labor leaders and representatives of working-class constituencies in Massachusetts and other states used the salutary effects of retirement on unemployment rates as one justification for state old age relief.[11]

Econometric research on retirement in postwar America

has focused on the stream of retirement income that the older worker sacrifices by delaying retirement and on the tax on earnings in the original Social Security provisions, a tax which penalized work. The econometric findings also show that even a relatively low ratio of benefits to previous earnings will prompt retirement.[12] Although OAA and insurance benefits were low in the 1930s and 1940s, so were earnings, particularly among older men in declining occupations and those seeking work, as subsequent sections of this chapter will indicate. Since workers could qualify for OAA without giving up their homes or declaring themselves paupers, they sacrificed a considerable stream of income from the state if they continued to work or look for work. Since only those without employment could qualify for OAA, and the original tax on earnings under Social Security insurance was high, the penalties for returning to work were severe.[13]

For older workers in low-paying jobs or jobs likely to be eliminated, for those thrown out of their regular jobs and looking for work, for those who were sick and trying to keep working, and for those with some assets who needed only the assurance of a small regular income, welfare benefits in the 1930s offered a new opportunity to *choose* more leisure. As the welfare state's retirement provisions became more and more generous, more and more workers found the alternative appealing. Without such welfare benefits, the majority of older men would probably have remained active members of the labor force. Instead, by 1940, they had fallen from a position of reduced but still powerful participation in the labor force to a distinct and peculiar nonworking status.

In Boston at least, declines in labor force activity cannot therefore be singled out as a sufficient cause for the rise of the welfare state; rather, the rise of the welfare state caused declines in labor force activity. A crisis with different causes might, however, have been brewing in the period 1890–1930.

Given relatively stable LFPR among older men, dependency rates in the older population (that is, the percentage of aged who could not support themselves) should not have increased markedly. Nonetheless, the absolute number of dependent old people increased as the older population increased in size. Fewer adult children were available to bear the responsibility of support, and this generation may have chafed under its duty. In addition, as the demographic data in Chapter II reveal, various subpopulations experienced special burdens.

Finally, the very constancy of the LFPR of older men suggests a new problem: between 1890 and 1930 the proportion of older men in the Boston labor force, and thus the number competing for jobs, increased regularly, with most of the increase (from 3.4 to 4.3 percent) occurring between 1920 and 1930. The crisis over old age and the campaign for state relief drew strength from the fact that both the dependent and the nondependent elderly populations had grown in size. Each of these groups warrants attention.

Female Workers
in Boston

For women, the relationship between work and the welfare state had an entirely different character. Before the Second World War, most older women who worked did so out of utter necessity. Since only the earliest censuses defined housewives as workers (a very meaningful decision),[14] older women displayed very low LFPR until our own time. During the period 1890–1940, women's participation rates peaked at ages 18–24, when about 65 percent worked. Marriage removed these women from the labor force. As they entered their thirties, a number of circumstances (e.g., widowhood) compelled women to return to paid work. Nonetheless, before the war, the LFPR of older women, especially married women, stayed low. Although aggregate female LFPR steadily increased across the period, and some changes occurred in the composition of the female labor force (larger proportions of married women worked), the truly striking changes have appeared since 1940. Although "the family life cycle" (marriage, empty nest, and so on) continues to influence women's work decisions, such influences have weakened in the postwar era, principally because the demand for women workers outstripped the available supply of 18- to 24-year-old single females. Hence, the recent period has witnessed profound increases in female LFPR, especially among older married women.[15]

Before the Second World War, older women in Boston worked more out of necessity than because demand appeared in the form of liberal wages and convenient hours. Their experiences were quite different from those of their male counterparts. During the period 1890–1930 in Boston, while the participation rate of men declined slightly, that of older women increased from 6 to 11 percent, as Table III-4 shows. Their proportion of the female labor force increased from 1 percent to nearly 3 percent. In the first characteristic older women followed the general, relatively slow, but steadily advancing participation of all women in the labor force. In Boston, the rising percentage of single women within the older female population (see Chapter II) also contributed to a high LFPR, since these women depended upon their own labor rather than familial resources. The welfare provisions of the 1930s and 1940s ended the steady increases in LFPR, which fell to about 10 percent, although the rates did not decline as sharply as men's did. Because older women were so much larger a part of Boston's population by 1950, their share of the labor force increased to 4 percent, despite declines in labor force activity.

Certainly the rising LFPR of older women before 1940 belies the conventional notion of declining labor force activity among the aged. But while the steady rates of males suggest their continued value as workers, the LFPR of women have a different meaning. In the next sections we will review the

Table III–4.
Labor Force Activity of Women 65 and Over, Boston, 1890–1950: Percentage of Female Population, Percentage of Female Labor Force, and LFPR

| | Females 65 and Over | | | Labor Force | | LFPR | | |
| | As % of Female Population | As % of Females 10 and Over | As % of Females 14 and Over | % 65 and Over | | 65 and Over | | Other Ages |
Census Year				Adjusted	Unadjusted	Adjusted	Unadjusted	Unadjusted
1890	4.3	5.2		1.1	1.2[a]	6.5	7.1[a]	25–44: 31.5
1900	4.2	5.1		1.3	1.4	7.7	8.4	24–44: 31.5
1910	4.6	5.6		NA	NA	NA	NA	NA
1920	5.0	6.1		1.9	2.0	9.9	10.8	25–44: 35.8[b]
1930	6.0	7.1		2.5	2.7	11.2	12.3	35–44: 30.8
1940	8.8		10.9	2.8[c]	2.8[c]	8.8	8.8	35–44: 32.7
1950[d]	10.8		13.5	4.0[c]	4.0[c]	10.4	10.4	35–44: 38.8

SOURCES: See Table III–1.

NOTE: The adjustment ratio for women 65 and over is 0.91353383. For all women it is 0.9735.

[a] Estimates from ratios in other age groups made because of census error; the *U.S. Census, 1890*, vol. 1, pt. 2, pp. 638–39, misreports the *total* number of women 65 and over with occupations.

[b] The 25–44 group includes all "age unknown" persons.

[c] In 1940 women 65 and over were 3.1 percent of all *employed* women not working on public emergency projects. In 1950 women 65 and over were 4.1 percent of all such employed women.

[d] Labor force and LFPR figures based on a 20 percent sample.

occupations that older men and women held. This analysis will show that for males occupational opportunities, while limited, were not closed, lending credence to the view that the Social Security Act had intentions and consequences not connected to the "need" of the older male worker.[16] But for older women, the labor market offered next to nothing, and the public welfare programs of the 1930s arrive in a more familiar guise, as angels of mercy.

Occupation and the Older Worker

Statistical series on labor force participation and proportion hardly suffice to convince a determined advocate of modernization or attitudinal theory that the work experience of the aged did not decline in the early twentieth century. Did the types of jobs older people could get change? Did certain occupations remain open to them, while others were closed? Were older men, defined as participating members of the labor force, reduced to pushing elevator levers or carrying out trash, after a lifetime of more prestigious work? The designation of occupations changed so much from one census to another that comparison across time provides less than reliable answers to such questions. But we are able to use specific occupational figures in two ways: first, we can make comparisons among occupations within any census year; second, where obvious consistency attended the occupational category, as in the case of carpenters or elevator operators, we can make comparisons over time.[17]

The following tables showing occupational distribution by age all reflect the cardinal fact of occupational categorization for older men and women: at any given time the aged are unevenly distributed among occupations: that is, compared with all workers, they are concentrated in some jobs and barely appear in others. The statistics for Boston demonstrate vividly that old age profoundly influenced what work one had. Whether this uneven distribution constituted "age discrimination" is not nearly so obvious.

Older Men
and Occupation

Tables III-5, III-6, and III-7 present statistics regarding specific occupations for male workers from 1890 through 1950. In each table the first row, "All occupations," provides the percentage of aged males in the labor force as a whole and allows the reader to estimate whether a specific occupation had the average percentage of older men or a larger or smaller one. I have divided occupations into general categories of white-collar, blue-collar, and service work, choosing job titles first for their comparability between censuses and second for their labor market significance. The occupations shown in these three tables cover about 40 percent of all male gainful workers (1890–1930) and employed men (1940 and 1950), and the same percentage of men 65 and over. (As noted above, censuses for 1940 and 1950 report only those actually employed.)

Regrettably, two categories of male workers could not be studied. The first includes most factory workers whose occupational titles were so fickle across censuses as to defy comparison. The second, the self-employed (e.g., small businessmen, wholesale dealers), suffered from the same mercurial shifts in occupational classification. Each category has a special significance claimed for it in this context: the first because the older worker is said to be especially disadvantaged in factory work; the second because high proportions of older men may report themselves as "employers and own-account workers."[18]

Table III-5 displays the percentages of men 65 and over in white-collar occupations, against a mean average of their percentage in all occupations at each census year. Certain occupations exhibit great continuity for older men; from 1890 to 1950, privileged white-collar occupations allowed

The Veterans of Labor

Table III–5.
Boston Males 65 and Over as a Percentage of Males in White-Collar Occupations, 1890–1950

	Census Year					
	Gainful Workers				Employed Workers	
Occupation	1890[a]	1900	1920	1930	1940	1950[b]
All Occupations[c]	3.1	3.0	3.6	4.5	4.4	5.9
Physicians, Surgeons	8.9	5.1	6.1	8.1	9.9	8.1
Lawyers, Judges	6.4	6.1	5.9	5.5	5.9	11.2
Bankers, Brokers	7.5	13.0	7.0	8.9	NA	11.3
Manufacturers, Manu-facturing Officials	7.6	8.3	6.0	8.2	8.3[d]	6.1
Bookkeepers[e]	1.2	2.3	3.6	4.6	3.4	4.0
Clerks		1.1	2.9[f]	2.8/3.0[g]	3.2[h]	4.4[f]
Salesmen	0.7	1.0	3.0	3.2	2.9	5.6
Insurance Agents	7.1[i]	6.5[i]	5.7	4.1	4.4	5.1

SOURCES: *U.S. Census, 1890,* vol. 1, pt. 2, p. 638; *U.S. Census, 1900, Special Reports . . . Occupations,* pp. 494–98; *U.S. Census, 1920,* vol. 4, pp. 1062–64; *U.S. Census, 1930,* vol. 4, pp. 728–30; *U.S. Census, 1940,* vol. 3, pt. 3, pp. 487–90; *U.S. Census, 1940,* vol. 2, pt. 21, pp. 208–10; and see Table III-1 and Edwards, *Comparative Occupation Statistics,* pp. 93, 95.

NOTE: Differences between gainful workers and employed workers are discussed in the text. The 1910 census did not publish occupational data for persons 65 and over in Boston.

[a] Unknown deleted from totals.

[b] Figures given are for Boston as a Standard Metropolitan Area (SMA).

[c] Unadjusted percentages for all occupations (white-collar, blue-collar, and service). Unadjusted figures must be used because adjustments cannot reasonably be made for specific occupations. In 1940 and 1950, however, figures are for *employed* men to correspond with those given for specific occupations (see Table III-1, note *a*).

[d] An important definitional change was made between 1930 and 1940. See Edwards, *Comparative Occupation Statistics,* pp. 35–48.

[e] Cashiers and accountants are sometimes included in this category.

[f] Includes all clerical work.

[g] Clerks in stores/clerks not in stores.

[h] "Other" clerks, the largest group.

[i] And other agents: claim, collection, etc. In 1930 insurance agents accounted for 31 percent of all types of agents included in this category in 1900 (Edwards, *Comparative Occupation Statistics,* p. 149).

the individual to work well beyond the average age. In banking and brokerage, for example, older men represented nearly 8 percent of the profession in 1890, against a general average of 3 percent; in 1950 older men made up over 11 percent of such financiers, while they composed less than 6 percent of the employed labor force as a whole. Older men in high-status white-collar occupations kept their positions more readily than other aged men.

Conversely, in low-status white collar work, which employed many more thousands, the percentage of aged men was not only lower, but substantially below the average for older men in the labor force as a whole, and particularly so in the earlier censuses. Old clerks and salesmen were a rarity at the turn of the century. In 1900 only one out of a 100 salesmen was aged, whereas three of every 100 workers in general had reached 65. But by 1950 older men were as well represented in sales as in the aggregate labor force. Taking low white-collar (LWC) work as a whole, the percentage of the aged in such occupations rose more rapidly than the percentage of older men in the entire labor force across the 60-year period. In a manner of speaking, the careers themselves aged. The rapid expansion of clerical work in the late nineteenth and early twentieth centuries drew into LWC work a youthful population (predominantly women). Several reasons may be advanced for youth's initial predominance: younger cohorts had more education, were more likely to be native-born and to speak English well and without accents, and might be cheaper to hire.[19] The aged did not meet these new occupational criteria well. However, having entered clerking, a young man might very well grow old within it; by 1920 and 1930 what had been exclusively young men's occupations (undoubtedly reinforced as such for a time by a belief that old people could not do the job)[20] were staffed by some older men as well. By this time older cohorts had education, job skills, and work histories that qualified them for clerical work. The aging of clerical occupations is the first in a series of signs that uneven age distributions in occupations were usually *temporary* and that youth itself was rarely an essential job requirement.

This cohort effect was understandably difficult to perceive at any moment. The uneven distributions of older workers among occupations—and their tendency to be overrepresented in obsolescent ones—led early twentieth-century observers as well as more recent commentators to perceive the aged worker as incapable of responding to the occupational challenges of "modern" society.[21] But as the analysis in this section demonstrates, many new occupations that at first employ only younger persons will, across time, exhibit larger proportions of older workers.

Data on blue-collar workers (Table III-6), while less manifest than that found in the distribution of older workers in white-collar occupations, confirm the pattern. Carpentry stands out for the sustained employment of older men. In all the censuses the percentage of carpenters who were 65 and over exceeded the percentage of older men in the whole labor force. Although the particular features of craftwork (skill, self pacing, and unionization) helped older men retain their places, the series for printers shows the inefficacy of these features in providing a guarantee of occupational access. The key, once again, is sudden change in occupational criteria. The very low percentage of printers 65 and over at the turn of the century (1.4 percent) reflected a complex combination of technological change, speed up, and union fear of unemployment that William Graebner has described.[22] However, printers soon experienced the same cohort effect as the clerks: by 1930 the proportion of older men in the printing trades exceeded the average for all workers. In 1935 a printers' union official from Worcester, Massachusetts, declared, "A man's knowledge of job printing is valuable until he drops."[23] Since the 1940 and 1950 figures represent only those actually employed, we know that a considerable proportion of working printers were older men.

Table III–6.
Boston Males 65 and Over as a Percentage of Males in Blue-Collar Occupations, 1890–1950

| Occupation | Census Year | | | | | |
| | Gainful Workers | | | | Employed Workers | |
	1890[a]	1900	1920	1930	1940	1950[b]
All Occupations[c]	3.1	3.0	3.6	4.5	4.4	5.9
Carpenters	5.0[d]	6.7	7.7	8.4	8.3	8.6
Laborers[e]	3.8	3.0	2.7[f]	3.3/4.3[g]	3.5	5.8
Machinists	2.6	2.5	2.0	4.0	5.0	5.3
Printers	1.4	1.7	3.4	5.2	6.1	6.7
Iron, Steel Workers[h]	2.1	2.3	2.6[i]	3.8	NA	NA
Truck Drivers	NA	NA	NA	0.7	1.0	1.3
Tailors	3.8	3.1	3.1	6.9	10.3	21.7

SOURCES: See Table III-5.

[a] Unknown deleted from totals.

[b] Figures given are for Boston as SMA.

[c] Unadjusted percentages for all occupations (white-collar, blue-collar, and service). Unadjusted figures must be used because adjustments cannot reasonably be made for specific occupations. For 1940 and 1950, however, figures are for *employed* men to correspond with those given for specific occupations (see Table III-1, note *a*).

[d] Total partly illegible in census.

[e] Since the definitions of specific types of laborers vary, I have combined categories except where noted.

[f] Building and general laborers; the figure for public service laborers is 5.4 percent.

[g] Building/general laborers.

[h] Both operatives and skilled workers (e.g., molders), except for 1920.

[i] Semiskilled operatives only.

The table for blue-collar work exposes a corollary to the rule of cohort effect. Occupations that were becoming obsolete tended to show rapidly increasing proportions of the aged across time, as the last cohorts trained in, accustomed to, or still working in them grew older.[24] Boston tailors are an example. In 1900 older men made up about 3 percent of all tailors and 3 percent of the labor force. In 1950, when elderly men were about 6 percent of the labor force, they accounted for almost 22 percent of tailors.

An incremental process of aging can be seen among machinists and iron and steel workers, but the changes in occupational definition in these categories place the evidence on a weak foundation. This is particularly unfortunate because we are denied a good historical picture of the impact of age in heavy industrial jobs, which might be quite distinct from other types in, for example, consistently denying the older man equal access. Within definitional limits, we can say for Boston that these occupations still demonstrate that the proportion of older workers increased in a specific occupation as the proportion of older men in the entire labor force increased. Here, as in Boston's aging population generally, we witness the results of the end of immigration: the labor force steadily aged, and, contrary to the conventional supposition, the share claimed by older workers within occupational categories once denied them steadily rose.

Table III-7 outlines those service occupations often seen as the old worker's last refuge.[25] Certain service occupations reflect cohort changes. For example, whereas aged men were underrepresented among personal servants in 1900 (1 percent, compared with a 3 percent average in the labor force), by 1950 they made up more than 14 percent of such servants (against a 6 percent average percentage in the labor force). By this period, personal service was a disappearing vocation. A similar trend can be observed in the tonsorial arts, whose practitioners were disproportionately young between 1890 and 1920, but in 1940 and 1950 exhibited very high percentages of aged workers (8 and 14 percent), a characteristic of declining occupations. By mid-century the aged exceeded average distributions in all these service occupations. Janitors, guards, and elevator operators appear to have been following old men's callings across the entire period 1890 to 1950. Whatever frank age bias existed in the labor market can be found in these low status service jobs, since it is

Table III–7.

Boston Males 65 and Over as a Percentage of Males in Service
Occupations, 1890–1950

| | Census Year | | | | | |
| | Gainful Workers | | | | Employed Workers | |
Occupation	1890[a]	1900	1920	1930	1940	1950[b]
All Occupations[c]	3.1	3.0	3.6	4.5	4.4	5.9
Janitors	9.4	6.8	12.3	11.8	8.1	15.7
Personal Servants	1.0	0.9	3.5	3.5	7.7	14.4
Barbers, Hairdressers	0.6	0.9	1.8	4.1	4.4	10.9
Guards, Watchmen	NA	NA	15.6	21.2	17.0[d]	17.9
Elevator Operators	NA	NA	6.6	10.7	6.9	17.5

SOURCES: See Table III-5.

[a] Unknown deleted from totals.

[b] Figures for Boston as SMA.

[c] Unadjusted proportions for all occupations (white-collar, blue-collar, and service). Unadjusted figures must be used because adjustments cannot reasonably be made for specific occupations. For 1940 and 1950, however, figures are for *employed* men to correspond with those given for specific occupations (see Table III-1, note *a*).

[d] The classification used in 1940 differs appreciably from that used in 1930; the presumption is that doorkeepers are included in this category in both censuses.

probable that men who could not hold on to work in their principal occupations fell into these secondary and ill-paid alternatives. But the refuge function of these occupations should not be exaggerated. In 1920 janitors, watchmen, and elevator operators made up 7 percent of gainful workers 65 and over; in 1950 this condition had hardly changed: only 8 percent of employed older men could be found in these occupations.

The distinction between gainful workers and the employed and the varying definition of occupations make precise characterization of the occupational experience of older men difficult. However, a broad view of the specific occupational roles of older men in Boston during the period from 1890 to 1950 leads to the following conclusions:

1. Older men were disproportionately distributed among occupations at every census, with low participation in newer fields.
2. Most occupations reviewed showed an increasing proportion of older men across the twentieth century, for two reasons:
   a. the proportion of aged men in the labor force as a whole increased, and
   b. within a few decades an occupation dominated by the young would show the effects of the aging of its practitioners: the proportion of older workers in it would increase more rapidly than their increase in the labor force as a whole.
3. High-status white-collar positions and low-status service jobs had extraordinarily high proportions of older men at all censuses.
4. Since precise job definition could not be achieved for factory workers, no judgment can be made about the occupational fate of the older members of the industrial working class.
5. Immigration restriction and the decline in native in-migration resulted in the aging of the labor force. Ironically, the age crisis of the 1920s and 1930s occurred in a period when the aged had a larger presence in most occupations than ever before.

In sum, it appears that older workers were threatened not by ageism but by rapid occupational change. Evidence for this conclusion can be found in early twentieth-century studies as well as in contemporary research. Elliot Dunlop Smith noted in 1929 the vulnerability of older workers in industries in which new methods were abruptly and sporadically introduced. Solomon Barkin's invaluable analysis of New York state manufacturing workers in 1930 strongly reinforces the reading that long-service aged employees did well and were valued by their employers, but that those seeking work faced great handicaps. William Graebner's study of the printing industry revealed the deleterious effects on the older worker of the sudden introduction of the linotype machine at the turn of the century.[26]

But when occupations and occupational requirements remained stable, older workers retained their positions within them, probably enjoying higher relative status than younger men. Older workers reduced turnover costs and thus increased productivity. They tended to be more stable and "responsible," were less likely to be disruptive or union-oriented, and were more dependent on their employers. We know that older men were generally wealthier, and, if recent findings can be applied to the early twentieth century, that the employer had good economic justification for pay scales that rewarded older workers more than younger ones, since such scales encouraged productivity in the latter group. On the whole, recent research suggests that the older male worker is a productive and *advantaged* worker in his regular job. There is no persuasive evidence that this was not the case in previous labor markets and the average older worker should not be presumed to be disadvantaged. However, recent research also demonstrates the negative consequences when an older worker loses his regular position and has to seek new work.[27] The aged workers in the early twentieth century faced similar difficulties in qualifying for new occupations. Since industrialization constantly provoked occupational change, the older worker who lost his job might well face a labor market in which his skills had become outmoded.

In an examination of discrimination against older workers in Massachusetts in the 1930s, the strongest evidence showed that such discrimination came into play when older workers *sought* employment. Barkin's New York study indicated that older men seeking to be rehired by their former employers were relatively successful, but those looking for work outside their regular trades did not fare well. The labor market studies of Herbert Parnes and his colleagues in the 1960s and 1970s offer similar evidence. Analyzing a large national sample of older men, Parnes found that the older worker generally commanded high status and pay in his work and was a valued employee. If, however, such a worker lost his job, he had much more difficulty regaining employment than younger men; the older worker's skills were often inappropriate for new occupations, and the expense of training older men was not a reasonable investment for an employer.[28]

The Boston evidence suggests that cohort effects—that is, the particular assets and liabilities of groups which are independent of age characteristics as such—must be considered before the true level of ageism can be measured. At any historical moment, the aged can be found to be underrepresented in "modern" occupations; but viewed across time, youthful cohorts in these occupations age, and the representation of aged workers within the occupations naturally increases. Failure to consider cohort effect leads to the conclusion that the particular moment chosen (usually between 1890 and 1930) marks the end of the utility of the aged worker or the point at which society found him useless. Insensitivity to cohort also obscures analysis of ageism or pure age discrimination, attributing to such prejudice a more permanent and universal force than the evidence will sustain.

Until analysis clearly shows otherwise, the aged workers of the pre–New Deal period should be assumed in most cases to be valued employees. Men in stable occupations, who held on to their principal calling, seem to have continued to participate actively in work and retained a prominent place in important trades. Indeed, one suspects that older workers brought to the workplace such valuable characteristics as skill, experience, and loyalty. For a minority of older men, however, work was less satisfying. If in obsolescent occupations, they were ill-paid and prone to unemployment; if they lost their jobs they probably had great difficulty in finding work, and the jobs they found might well be in the lowest sectors of service work.

This minority of men leads us to a discussion of the majority of working women. Although cohort effects influenced female occupational experience as well, other factors, specific to women, had much greater impact. For most older women, the world of work was grim indeed.

Older Women
and Occupation

Table III-8 presents data on women's occupations similar to those developed for men's work. That these can be summarized in one table provides the first fact in the analysis: women did not enjoy the variety of occupations available to men. In 1900 the occupations listed in Table III-8 represented more than 70 percent of all working women and more than 70 percent of those 65 and over. In 1950 the listed occupations employed about 60 percent of each group. The first row displays the average percentage of the female labor force that was 65 and over (about 1 percent in 1890 and about 4 percent in 1950) and provides the standard by which the aged can be judged to be over- or under-represented in a particular occupation.

Women's occupations replicate several of the findings for men: the disproportionate distribution by age at any single census; cohort effects as occupations age; and the predominance of older workers in obsolete occupations. There are, however, several important differences. Perhaps the most salient is that the traditional duties of marriage strongly affected the occupational fortunes of women workers: when an older woman entered the labor market, her principal training usually consisted of decades of housework.[29] The marital experience provided older working women (usually

The Veterans of Labor

Table III–8.
Boston Females 65 and Over as a Percentage of Females in
Various Occupations, 1890–1950

	Census Year					
	Gainful Workers				Employed Workers	
Occupation	1890[a]	1900	1920	1930	1940	1950[b]
All Occupations[c]	1.2[d]	1.4	2.0	2.7	3.1	4.1
Nurses—Trained	5.0[e]	2.8[e]	0.6	1.0	1.0	3.1
—Practical			3.9[e]	7.3[e]	4.5[e]	15.0[e]
Boarding/Lodging House and Hotel Keepers	5.8	7.2	10.0	12.6	20.8	—[f]
Housekeepers	5.7	4.9	10.3	12.7	10.9[g]	15.2[h]
Servants	0.8	1.1[i]	3.3	4.5	6.7[g]	15.0
Dressmakers		1.3[i]	7.0[k]	13.4[k]	11.3[k]	16.0[k]
Seamstresses	0.9	3.3[i]				
Milliners		0.6[i]	NA	NA	NA	NA
Tailoresses	0.8[i]	1.3[i]	3.7	6.0	NA	NA
Bookkeepers[l]	0.1	0.3	0.4	0.6	1.3	2.4
Clerks	0.2	0.4	0.4	0.8/1.1[m]	1.7[n]	1.7[n]
Stenographers, Typists	0.0	0.1	0.1	0.2	0.9	1.1
Saleswomen	0.1	0.2	0.6	1.0	1.5	3.3/3.1[o]
Teachers[p]	0.6	1.4	2.3	3.2	4.2	4.5
Clothing Factory Operatives	0.3[q]	NA	2.0	3.0	1.5[r]	2.7

SOURCES: *U.S. Census, 1890*, vol. 1, pt. 2, pp. 638–39; *U.S. Census, 1900, Special . . . Occupations*, pp. 498–90; *U.S. Census, 1920*, vol. 4, pp. 1064–65; *U.S. Census, 1930*, vol. 4, pp. 730–31; *U.S. Census, 1940*, vol. 3, pt. 3, p. 491; *U.S. Census, 1950*, vol. 2, pt. 21, p. 210 and see Table III-1; Edwards, *Comparative Occupation Statistics*, pp. 19–86, 87–174.

[a] Unknown deleted from totals.

[b] Figures given are for Boston as SMA.

[c] Unadjusted proportions for all occupations. Unadjusted figures must be used because adjustments cannot reasonably be made for specific occupations. For 1940 and 1950, however, figures are for *employed* women to correspond with those given for specific occupations (see Table III-4, note c).

[d] Estimated (see Table III-4, note a).

[e] Includes midwives. The classification used in 1940 is appreciably different from that used in 1930.

[f] See figures for housekeepers.

widows) with skill in cleaning, cooking, watching children, and practical nursing. Such abilities were ill-rewarded in the labor market and increasingly obsolescent by the early twentieth century. When a widow had to go to work, she suffered the public consequences of years of training in private domestic service.

We have seen that older women shared with all women increasing participation in the labor force. The LFPR of older women did not increase as rapidly as that of other female age groups, but among employed women in 1940 and 1950, participation exceeded that reported among gainful workers in 1890 and 1900. Because of rising participation and the larger proportional size of the older female age group by mid-century, women 65 and over constituted nearly four times as high a percentage of the female labor force as they had at the turn of the century. (In both periods this percentage was rather small, ranging from extremes of 1 percent to 4 percent.) Without government welfare, the post–World War II figures would have climbed still higher.

---

[g] Edwards argues (*Comparative Occupation Statistics,* p. 30) that 1930 and 1940 figures for housekeepers are not comparable. But the error lies in misassignment of servants to housekeeper status; therefore, these two rows may be combined to compare 1930 to 1940.

[h] Not in private households; presumably includes the boarding or lodging house and hotel keepers previously separately classified.

[i] Includes waitresses.

[j] Census does not indicate whether factory work is included; it is likely that factory and nonfactory sewing were combined.

[k] Not in factories. Enumerators often erred in distinguishing these clothing makers from those employed by factories. The classification used in 1940 is appreciably different from that used in 1930. Edwards, *Comparative Occupation Statistics,* p. 30.

[l] Cashiers and accountants sometimes included.

[m] Clerks not in stores/clerks in stores.

[n] "Other" clerical workers, the largest group.

[o] "All" saleswomen/retail saleswomen.

[p] Includes college personnel.

[q] All textile manufacturing operatives.

[r] The classification used in 1940 differs appreciably from that used in 1930.

Older female workers were very unevenly distributed among the occupations. Once again our initial observation is that age skews distribution. And, again, the next finding is that such an effect is temporary.

These rules of thumb are illustrated in the category of saleswomen. In 1890 and 1900 older women simply did not do sales work (0.1 and 0.2 percent). We might presume, as did some of those who hired sales workers at this time, that selling was by its nature a young woman's profession. But each census showed the expansion of the proportion of older women in such jobs. As early as 1929 sales was recognized as a field in which older women were accepted.[30] By 1950 the proportion of saleswomen who were 65 and over very nearly equalled the average proportion of older women among all employed women. Trained nurses followed the same pattern. In 1920, when training for nursing was no more than 30 years old, very few women 65 and over could be found among trained nurses. By 1950 they had come close to parity (3 percent, compared with a 4 percent share of the employed labor force). Once again what appears to be ageism may be judgment based on a proper and rational criterion: training.[31] Aged women, like aged men, suffered a great liability when occupational criteria changed; often they could not qualify. But this lack of qualifications was an accident of age, not its direct consequence.

Teaching showed a similar transition. In 1890 older women made up about half their expected fraction among teachers; by 1920 they exceeded their share; and in 1950, 4.5 percent of all employed teachers were 65 and over, compared with 4.1 percent of employed women in general. The aging of this profession follows the cohort pattern and may be especially influenced by the large number of single women in Boston: traditionally a young women's occupation in the nineteenth century, teaching attracted young, well-educated, and career-minded women at the turn of the century, many of whom continued to work in the profession as they grew older.[32]

The rule of cohort effect is not, however, perfectly followed. Other white-collar occupations were slow to change. Older women clearly increased their share in bookkeeping, clerical, and typing jobs across the period but remained well below equal representation in 1950, suggesting a persistent age bias. Bookkeepers, a bare tenth of the average in 1890, had reached 60 percent of it in 1950 (2.4 versus 4.1) Clerks and stenographer/typists showed less progress, although after 1950 clerical work became a major occupation of older women.

Practical nursing exemplified the corollary to the rule of cohort effect: as a declining, obsolescent occupation, its ranks became quite aged. By 1950 fully 15 percent of all practical nurses were 65 and over, compared with about 4 percent of employed women in general. The needle trades, the traditional occupations of women forced into the labor market at the turn of the century, followed the same pattern. The 1890 census showed remarkably few older women among those sewing, despite the turn-of-the-century stereotype of the poor widow at her needlework, because of the true predominance of younger sewing women, but also because of the notorious failure of census enumerators to count accurately women who worked at home and the reluctance of some older women to admit that they sewed for pay.[33] In 1900 the census takers showed more precision in dividing up the sewing trades, and their efforts revealed that older women who sewed found work in the least remunerative needlework category, that of "seamstress," where they exceeded their average percentage in the labor force (3.3 versus 1.4 percent). Younger women dominated millinery, tailoring, and dressmaking, higher-status and higher-paid sewing occupations. In 1920 the census also separated factory sewing from nonfactory work, and the percentage of older women trying to work out of their homes was revealed to be quite large (7 percent). By this time the general decline of handsewing as a female occupation was evident in the rising percentage of older women still trying to make a living at it: in 1950 older women made up 16 percent of all non-factory seamstresses, four times their average representation in the labor force. Not a field for the old at the turn of the century, sewing was an old woman's calling fifty years later.

The latter result reflected more than the aging of women who had entered a once promising trade in their youth. The concentrations of older women in handsewing and similar jobs denoted the persistence of a school of outmoded training: that is, the cultivation of traditional skills during marriage. The figures for household service expose this second effect with still more force. In Boston the underrepresentation of older women in household service was reversed between 1890 and 1950 (0.8 percent versus 15 percent). In addition to women who grew old in this vocation, widows and other women who had lived most of their lives as wives and thus as unpaid housekeepers found themselves thrust out into the labor market with only the skills learned around home and hearth.[34] Younger women, eager to enter new occupations with higher pay, more status, and some future, disdained household service. White-collar work became increasingly important, and young, educated, native-born women beginning work tended to enter these new, more attractive, and better-paid occupations.[35] Older women remained concentrated in the older occupations. In the first place, many older female workers were products of an earlier labor market: they began their work lives when sewing and domestic service constituted the principal occupations of all women, and their training and work histories prepared them for such jobs. Often foreign-born, poorly educated, and lacking language skills, they did not bring strong credentials to the clerical labor market. But older women were also likely to be found in low status jobs because when widows had to enter the labor force they qualified for tasks in which they had trained, in which they had been working, and by which they had earned their private keep: housework, sewing, cooking, and practical nursing.[36]

In 1890 domestic service was the listed occupation of 34 percent of all women, a major vocation indeed, and one in which many young women participated. Among older female gainful workers, 24 percent listed domestic service as their calling, a sizable group though considerably less than the female average. A decline began in 1900, and by 1940 only 9 percent of all employed women worked as domestic servants. It is obvious from these statistics and from a wealth of other evidence that service was not a profession in which young women were interested. But 19 percent of women 65 and over, or nearly one in every five, remained employed as domestics. Trained in their youth in service work, either in regular employment or as housewives, older women maintained a high profile in domestic service.[37]

The special influence of the domestic experience of widows can be seen among boarding or lodging house keepers and housekeepers. Between 1890 and 1950 the percentage of them who were 65 and over steadily increased from about 6 to 15 percent. In 1890 such jobs accounted for only 2 percent of the labor force, but 11 percent of all gainful workers 65 and over were employed in them. In 1940 this occupation again provided jobs for 2 percent of the female labor force, but now 14 percent of all employed women 65 and over claimed them. In that year fully one-fifth of all boarding house, lodging house, and hotel keepers were 65 and over. The unusual marital circumstances of these women reveal the source of their "training." In 1900 widowed and divorced women of any age made up 11 percent of Boston's female labor force, but 52 percent of those who ran boarding and lodging houses and 26 percent of the housekeepers. In 1930 the widowed and divorced constituted 12 percent of the female labor force, but 32 percent of boarding and lodging house keepers and 40 percent of housekeepers. For women without husbands, most of whom were aged, boarding and lodging house management remained a steady area of employment, not only because it used the skills a wife learned in her work at home, but also because it often used her principal asset, the house.[38]

This examination of older women's occupational status can be summarized by restating six principal points.

1. The occupations open to older women were extremely limited in the period from 1890 to 1950, a disadvantage shared to a lesser degree by women of all ages.
2. Older women increased both their LFPR and their proportion in the female labor force during this time.
3. Jobs at any census were unevenly distributed by age. Older women, disproportionately concentrated in some jobs, had almost no representation in others, especially the newer occupations.
4. But new jobs showed the cohort effect noted for men's occupations. The proportion of older women in occupations such as sales work, negligible in 1900, increased more rapidly than the proportion of older women in the labor force as a whole, suggesting the aging of the participants. Certain clerking occupations, however, were more resistant to this change.
5. Occupations that declined in importance or became obsolescent showed the same aging process in a more dramatic form as older women, who had begun their work lives in these jobs, became more and more heavily represented among participants.
6. But older women paid a penalty not incurred by their male peers. They were lodged in declining occupations also because these were "domestic" in nature; their training and experience as wives prepared them for such work, or, conversely, their lack of training and investment in newer occupational skills while married[39] made it difficult for them to secure good places when forced into the labor market.

Conclusion:
Working, 1890–1950

In this chapter we have considered the proportion and participation of older workers in Boston's labor force and their fortunes within specific occupations. The period from 1890 to 1930 witnessed no significant decline in the participation rates of older people; and their proportionate weight in the city's labor force increased. These findings run counter to the conventional view that their labor force activity fell sharply throughout the twentieth century. After 1930 participation rates did fall dramatically, very likely as a direct consequence of welfare legislation.

Why did the participation rates remain relatively steady before 1930 in an economically advanced area like Boston? In light of the effects of New Deal welfare legislation, the most satisfactory single answer is that a certain proportion of older people *had* to work. No broad welfare system encouraged retirement. Urban participation rates always remained below rural ones because rural rates are artifically inflated and because increased wealth allowed a larger percentage of urban industrial workers to "retire." In addition, age discrimination and rapid changes in occupational criteria pushed some men out of work sooner than they would have chosen. In comparison with the relatively constant occupational demands of farm work, the urban labor market often demanded new skills and training; the older worker out of a job, or in a declining trade, had little chance of qualifying for such jobs. From data analyzed in Chapter II, it appears that some of these men and women became dependent on their relatives for support. But most men were workers and their occupational record indicates that they could compete in the pre-welfare labor market.

Theories of ageism, modernization effects, and so on all imply that judgments against older workers (whether based on legitimate criteria or mere prejudice) lowered the demand for their services: hence, their LFPR declined. But if social security induces workers to retire, lower participation rates can be explained as the result of reductions in supply. Reductions in supply mean at least partly voluntary action by workers who choose more leisure and some income over little leisure and more income. When we consider the very great satisfaction that retirees report with their status and the current popularity of early retirement, the idea that workers have been forced out is not completely persuasive.[40]

The discovery of steady participation in Boston does not mean that all the aged prospered before the New Deal. We have seen that older workers were often caught in inferior, poorly paid occupations, and we have no sure knowledge of their levels of unemployment before 1940. But the evidence presented does require that we carefully reassess the status of the aged worker in this period. We have assumed forced retirement, the closure of "modern" occupations, and a steady, irreversible decline in the fortunes of the aged. These assumptions should be discarded, and tests of hypotheses should replace them.

Another thesis drawn from the evidence states, first, that occupations are always unevenly distributed by age and, second, that the particular pattern of distribution is temporary: occupations with low percentages of old people will in subsequent censuses show higher percentages. Cohorts that in their youth enjoyed access to certain occupations will display continued ability to work in them in old age. Ignoring this cohort effect exaggerates the significance of the occupational age distribution at any one historical moment and treats age discrimination as a more complete and permanent phenomenon than the data will support. Certainly age discrimination did exist. Evidence of defamation of the aged worker can be found at every turn in the early twentieth century. As William Graebner has argued, the very concept of "retirement" implies discrimination by age.[41] However, some decisions that injured the aged were based on cohort rather than age deficiencies: education, language abilities, previous work experience. These deficiencies may be rational criteria for an employer, and we should differentiate between such criteria and "ageism." Even the low rate of return to training an older worker, while based purely on age and perhaps discriminatory, represents a form of rational calculation by employers which does not impugn the abilities of older workers.

The evidence from Boston suggests that the most important impediment to the employment of older workers was rapid change. That is, older male workers probably enjoyed what they command today: authority, high pay, and satisfaction in their work. But these conditions depended on retaining positions in occupations with stable job requirements. When new occupations emerged, job requirements changed suddenly, or unemployment struck, the older worker was especially vulnerable.

Older women suffered from still another liability. Those who returned to the labor force after lives as wives and mothers found gainful employment a drab rerun of their marital domestic service. Trained in domestic skills that the market did not value, such women swelled the ranks of occupations related to those skills: service, sewing, and practical nursing. These promised little in pay or future.

The principal contention of the chapter has been that older people in Boston were *working* people before social security, and that older men worked in occupations that gave them dignity and independence. But demographic and occupational data have also revealed a significant minority of older Bostonians who were dependent or working in occupations that provided little defense against destitution. It is these elders who symbolized the old age crisis and it is to their story that we now turn.

Chapter IV
The Private
Charity System

The development of welfare for the aged preoccupies researchers, doubtless because welfare stands out as the signal characteristic of life for the elderly today. Despite fervent disagreement about the cause of the decline in the status of older persons, attitudinalists and modernizationists share a deterministic view of the rise of the welfare state: a belief that the Social Security Act was a *necessary* response to the relentless deterioration of the life of older people.

In fact, the welfare state was never inevitable. Such a view obscures a rich heritage of class and ethnic conflict over whether such a system should be created. The majority of Boston's aged probably enjoyed relatively stable, rewarding, and independent lives before the New Deal. Nonetheless, poverty attended a significant minority, and some relied wholly on their children and relatives, many of whom were themselves poor. As we shall see, those without money or family made up the truly unfortunate, the men and women likely to become the clients of public or private relief agencies.

The fate of the minority who received assistance provides a clear picture of urban people who lost independent status and identifies the factors that precipitated dependency. In addition, an examination of public and private welfare reveals a struggle over the future relationship between the elderly and the state, one with direct implications for the aged who relied on their families for support. The openly impoverished aged—the clients of charity—became the symbols of the "struggle for social security." But the covertly dependent, the aged who relied not on charity but on family, played the more important part in the origins of the welfare state.

In this chapter and the two that follow, I contrast two prominent private charities with Boston's public welfare system, using case records as well as institutional materials. The private institutions—the Home for Aged Women (HAW), founded in 1849, and the Home for Aged Men (HAM), founded in 1861—reflect the character of private charity before the New Deal. Their directors and social workers forcefully espoused a modern and persuasive ideology of welfare that was ultimately defeated in the Social Security Act, and the beneficiaries of these charities represent the successes and failures of the private alternative to public relief. In contrast, Boston's municipal system reveals the strengths and weaknesses of public relief, and its leaders, drawn from the working-class and ethnic constituencies of Boston, expressed a radically different view of what welfare should be.

The two Homes were founded before the Civil War by the Boston merchant elite, later known as the Brahmins. The institutions sprang out of two important antebellum phenomena: the creation of new welfare systems by American urban elites, and virulent nativism. Indeed, the founders wedded these nineteenth-century concerns: they formulated and imposed a punitive welfare system on the working classes of Boston and then established these private homes to rescue impoverished Yankees from that public system because it had filled up with foreigners. Following a blunt and intelligent welfare ideology, antebellum elites constructed the rationale of American benevolence: charity ruined the poor, stealing their self-reliance and undermining their work ethic; denial of aid was thus the greater charity. From this viewpoint, the possibility of a penurious old age was a necessary spur to youthful initiative.[1]

The twentieth-century directors and social workers of the Homes preserved much of this ideology. As agents of the traditionally conservative and Protestant private charity system of Boston, they emphasized the need for careful investigation of all clients. Their social workers used casework methods to discourage reliance on relief rather than family, consistently opposed the expansion of public welfare programs, and attacked the movement for state pensions for the elderly in the 1920s.[2] They were, nonetheless, among the first Americans to recognize the special needs of the aged and give them aid.

The Founding Fathers

Only certain elders deserved the founders' benevolence. Although both of these institutions sought a modicum of "respectability" in candidates for aid, and advanced age, proven indigency, and Boston residence were stipulated requirements, for each the cardinal rule was that the candidate be American-born.

The HAW was the first charity for the aged established by the set of elite reformers who had restructured the administration and function of welfare in antebellum Boston. By the late 1840s the attention of Boston reformers had begun to center on the immigrant poor, and a violent reaction to "aliens" was the source of the HAW and the HAM. In 1848 a Boston delegation undertook a study of other cities' welfare institutions. Impressed by old age homes for women in New York and Philadelphia, prominent Bostonians successfully petitioned the city for land to benefit a class of poor "whose situation entitles them to peculiar sympathy," many of them "our own countrywomen" who, without such a charity, might drop "to the level of almshouse inmates and paupers." For the city almshouse these women had a "natural repugnance which we cannot but respect in the poor of our own people,—a repugnance to be herded with paupers of every character, condition and clime." Among the petitioners were the directors of the Boston almshouse. On 30 April 1849 an act of incorporation was approved for the "Association for the Relief of Indigent Females."[3]

If there remained any doubt about the reasons for the founding of this asylum, it was laid to rest at the opening of the Home on Charles Street on 1 May 1850. President Henry B. Rogers praised the Christian character and breadth of New England charity and lamented the disruption of that benevolence by the influx of "great masses . . . from other states and countries," strangers "foreign to our modes of thought—to our habits of industry and thrift,—and to that self-education and discipline" that forestalled poverty. Foreigners had "taken possession of the public charities . . . as they have of the houses where our less privileged classes formerly resided." The native and foreign populations could not be assisted in "homogeneous institutions," for "they form two distinct classes which are so entirely separated by education, temperament, and mental and religious prejudices, that they refused to be associated together indiscriminately." The Home was designed to aid the "bone of our bone, and flesh of our flesh."[4]

The founders of the HAM used precisely the same phrase 10 years later. They asked a candid question of fellow Yankees in a city besieged by poor Irish Catholic immigrants: "who could think of our respectable aged but indigent American men being compelled" to drop to "the level of almshouse inmates and paupers?"[5]

Established by the same Bostonian elite and imbued with the same nativistic ideology, the HAW and HAM designated similar rules. The HAW required that its beneficiaries be American-born women at least 60 years of age, Boston residents for the last 10 years, and the possessors of satisfactory testimonials to the "respectability of their character and the propriety of their conduct." A Committee on Admissions was enjoined to "visit the applicants and inquire into their circumstances and character," making a full report "of all the material facts in each case." But nativity remained the central requirement, and the blatant xenophobia of this Home was to continue well into the twentieth century. In early 1851 the first foreigner was "rejected on account of her Foreign birth:—Mrs. Wright, a very worthy & deserving woman, personally." Such rejections were often noted in the records. In the 1920s the correspondence of the Committee on Admissions reveals the emphasis on American and New England "stock," though correspondents were privately advised that English parentage would not be damning.[6] The officers of the HAM, while equally nativistic and governed by similar requirements, also showed a precocious understanding of the problems for aging men that had already arisen in their city and were eventually to afflict the whole of industrial America. The earliest records employed the phrase "having seen better days" to describe the ideal client. Although a common and straightforward expression of class consciousness, the phrase reflected as well an awareness of the risks of sudden loss among older men in an urban environment. Founders initially described the charity as one for men "past the active business and duties of life," who, "in consequence of reverses" and "misfortune," found themselves without means. In 1866 the annual report asked for sympathy for men "who after their period of lucrative employment find themselves impoverished. Vicissitudes happen to all; and if fortune generally attends efforts well directed, its gifts are not to be controlled."[7] This understanding of risk, while not applicable to the Irish working class, signaled the realization among these businessmen that life off the farm might be precarious indeed:

> 'Tis the wink of an eye, 'tis the draught of a breath,
> From the blossom of health, to the paleness of death.[8]

The early officers understood the hazards of old age for men in Boston and made provision for dependency among old Yankees, even as the stern precepts of their welfare ideology forbade special provision for other aged people. Although the founders believed that they would be serving a very special class of fallen gentlemen, who deserved such indulgence, they never served this group at all. By examining the case records of the men they did aid, and of the women relieved by the HAW, we can discover which elders actually needed help, and what the reasons for their dependency were.

The Clients
of the Homes

By the twentieth century the HAW and the HAM figured as the centerpieces in a limited display of Boston charities providing relief to the aged. Both were large and well-endowed institutions, each housing as many as fifty residents and assisting others in their own lodgings. The outside aid department of the HAM gave relief to more than a hundred men; Christine McLeod, one of the first American social workers to work with the aged, directed the department and wielded considerable authority in the Boston debate over welfare provisions for the aged.

In 1925 only 17 private old age homes existed in Boston. They were one element of an ostensibly secular, but really quite Protestant, private welfare system created in the nineteenth century, which not only dominated private relief efforts, but strove to control the city's public relief and exercised great influence over the state Department of Public Welfare. The Catholic archdiocese, representing the ethnic working-class constituencies of Boston, maintained several old age homes and relief societies, but Catholic influence was more powerfully expressed in its constituencies' political control over city welfare funds.[9]

The HAM and HAW illustrate the dominant character of

private relief for the aged poor before the New Deal. Their excellent case records offer an opportunity to examine the experience of a particular type of impoverished older person, to assess the capacity of private relief to respond to the problem of dependency in old age, and to search out the sources of the demand for public social security. Although our discussion will focus on the period from 1900 to 1950, certain nineteenth-century materials illuminate the development of private American charity. Samples were taken of the case records of "clients" (i.e., persons who received aid inside or outside the institution) during three periods: the 1900s, the 1920s, and the 1940s; from the HAW 180 case records were selected, from the HAM, 164.[10] Each institution kept meticulous records, providing information in almost precisely the same form from the 1840s or 1860s to the 1940s. Each record contained the applicant's name, date of application, type of aid requested (admission or outside aid), date of birth, place of birth, marital history, and occupational history. Means of support, property, physical condition, and religion were noted, and the applicants were required to give the names and addresses of children and other relatives. (Education was never an item on application forms.) The HAW additionally supplied data on parental birthplaces, father's occupation, husband's name, birthplace, date and place of death, and occupation, and joint property held at the time of his death. Although applicants had reason to exaggerate their dependency and the limitations of their family networks, the homes required recommending letters and interviews, and after 1920 both employed social workers to investigate applicants.

The case records indicate first that the homes vigorously maintained in the twentieth century the ethnocentric biases upon which they were founded (see Table IV-1). It is clear from the distribution that the directors of the homes aided men and women of their own "stock," the rural New Eng-

105

Table IV–1.
Birthplaces of HAW and HAM Clients, 1900–1950

Birthplace	HAW (%)		HAM (%)	
Boston	27		22	
Other Massachusetts	22	81 New	22	74 New
Maine	16	England	14	England
Other New England	16		16	
Other United States	7		7	
Foreign	12		19	
Total	100		100	
	(n = 179)		(n = 159)	

SOURCES: Sample of 180 clients of HAW (one case missing birthplace data) and 164 clients of HAM (five missing data).

landers to whose villages the Boston rich resorted each July and August. A few clients hailed from urban places in these rural regions, but most reported farm or small-town origins. These country cousins, who migrated to Boston from rural Massachusetts, Maine, and New Hampshire, were the chief beneficiaries of the HAW and HAM throughout the twentieth century.

At the HAW, even in the last cohort studied (the 1940s), 67 percent of the beneficiaries were New England–born; and in the 1900s that figure was 97 percent. At the turn of the century, 42 percent came from the two states of Maine and New Hampshire; the singular role of these states highlights the rural, upper New England background of the beneficiaries of this Brahmin charity.

After 1876 the HAW also required information regarding parental nativity, and these data reaffirm the ethnic bias of the charity. As late as the 1940s, 62 percent of the clients' mothers and fathers had been born in New England. Maritime Canada, Scotland, and England accounted for about three quarters of the small proportion with foreign parentage. Foreign birth among clients themselves was exceedingly rare, and of the 21 foreign-born women admitted, aided, or approved in the 50-year period, 19 came from Maritime Canada or England.

At the HAM antagonism to other ethnic and religious groups surfaced regularly in the records. Of the 19 percent of all clients in the 1900–1950 sample who were foreignborn, more than half were from England or the Maritime Provinces of Canada. Of 16 rejected applications with complete information, 11 were from foreign-born men. Catholic and foreign-born men who did receive aid were often special cases: John Bogue, born in Ireland, was at first rejected, but when it was learned that he had nursed the prominent Brahmin, Charles Francis Adams, he was granted aid. One was well-advised to claim, as Patrick Danis did, that he was born a Catholic through no fault of his own. Case records and social workers' reports often emphasized that an applicant was from "good New England stock," or "a gentlemen of the old school and an 'American.'"[11] Although the distribution of birthplaces among HAM clients changed across time, no shift away from British ethnicity occurred. By the 1940s the percentage of foreign-born had increased to 27 percent of the cohort, compared with 13 percent of the 1900s cohort. But these foreigners, like those of the HAW, hailed from an extension of the New England social order—the Canadian Maritimes—or from England itself. The low percentage of foreign-born in the client populations, and especially the absence of Irish old people, is especially striking in view of the demographic characteristics of Boston's aged population discussed in Chapter II. Although the migrants and immigrants whom the Homes served were a select ethnic group, they did represent an important subpopulation in early twentieth-century Boston. The men and women of these two Homes were part of a vast movement of New Englanders (as the officers put it, "the great numbers from our rural districts"] who moved to the city to find work and who, in their advanced years, found destitution.[12]

Although the occupations secured by this population group in their youth generally surpassed those of their Irish and Italian coevals,[13] these jobs offered no absolute guarantee against dependency in old age. Despite the intention of the Yankee homes to serve a "better class" of the indigent, the occupational backgrounds of clients and their families indicate blue-collar and low white-collar characteristics. For men aided by the HAM, occupational data make it evident that the goal of serving the fallen upper classes was never realized. Rather, even in the nineteenth century, the Home served a "respectable" but working-class clientele. By the twentieth it was quite apparent that the charities of the Home were rarely extended to a Brahmin who had fallen from grace, as President Charles E. Rogerson lamented in 1911:

> We find it increasingly difficult to select applicants for either admission to the Home or for outside aid who come within [our] restrictions. We admit and aid outside men who have been mechanics, salesmen and carpenters. . . . I presume we shall have to rest content to aid this class of men to the exclusion of that other class for which the Home was originally intended, that is, indigent merchants, because the changed conditions do not bring to our attention such applicants.[14]

However disconcerting this may have been to Rogerson, the occupational backgrounds of the HAM clients and applicants reward present research by providing insights into the general problem of dependency among old people: whereas many poor older people had always been poor, the HAM tried to aid men with above-average backgrounds. The incidence of old age dependency among the once "respectable" was a growing concern in Massachusetts and other states in the early twentieth century.[15] Although the HAM did not relieve the fallen rich, it did aid men from somewhat higher

Table IV–2.
Principal Occupation of HAM Clients by Cohort and Demicentury

	Cohorts			
Occupation	*1900s (%)*	*1920s (%)*	*1940s (%)*	*1900–1950 (%)*
LBC	14	6	15	13
SBC	22	26	22	23
LWC	40	47	35	40
MWC	24	21	28	25
	(n = 55)	(n = 34)	(n = 68)	(n = 157)

NOTE: Seven cases missing occupational data; rounding errors cause deviations from 100 percent in totals for columns.

occupational groups than those described in public welfare records, and its cases thereby reveal the broad characteristics of the loss of independence in old age. The HAM required the applicant to list his principal occupation as well as that currently held. I have grouped these occupations into five categories: none, low blue-collar (LBC), skilled blue-collar (SBC), low white-collar (LWC), and middle white-collar (MWC).[16]

Table IV-2 displays the distribution of principal occupations among clients between 1900 and 1950. The HAM could justly be called a clerks' charity. The percentage in LWC (largely clerking jobs) contrasts sharply with much smaller percentages of LWC workers in Boston's aggregate aged population (see Chapter III, Table III-5). Very few of the beneficiaries worked in the LBC category that one would expect to be most susceptible to dependency in old age. Allowing for the poor pay attending some LWC occupations,[17] about half of those receiving aid between 1900 and 1950 had been in moderately well-paid principal occupations. These occupational patterns remain remarkably stable across time.

Over 60 percent of the men in each cohort came from white-collar occupations, and about one-third from blue-collar work. However, these categories do not exist *in vacuo*. Census data on occupation are not controlled for age and ethnicity, but such data as exist suggest that HAM occupations mirror the relatively advantaged occupational distribution of the Yankee/British ethnic group from which beneficiaries were drawn.[18] Although the beneficiaries had almost never achieved upper-middle class status, their stable and respectable occupational histories confirm the impression of contemporary observers that "respectable" occupations did not guarantee security in old age.

How did these men fall from independence to dependence? Since the HAM recorded both principal callings and jobs held at the time of application, we are provided with a measure of stability of occupation. Tamara K. Hareven, echoing the analysis of investigators in the 1920s, has argued that aging men were forced into menial jobs:

> in the last years of their lives, even highly skilled workers were forced into temporary jobs in unskilled occupations, after having spent the better part of their lives in efforts to move up the ladder. . . . The major transition in the work life was . . . not necessarily the complete termination of the individual's work career, but often the move to a temporary, semi-skilled or unskilled job while still in his forties or early fifties.[19]

Caroline Hoppe and Judith Treas likewise find evidence of downward economic mobility among the residents of a Los Angeles retirement home.[20] In 1925 the Massachusetts Commission on Pensions argued that older men were unable to maintain their regular occupations after the age of 65: "many men in old age had been forced to give up their regular work in mills and factories and to become elevator men and janitors." The commission's conclusion was hardly warranted by the tabular results presented: of 2,818 men who reported few assets and little income, 14 had worked as elevator tenders and 41 as janitors in their principal occupations. In listing present occupations, 23 men identified themselves as tenders and 58 as janitors; therefore, these secondary occupations provided job opportunities for less than 1 percent of the indigent population surveyed.[21]

Among the old men aided by the HAM—of whom very few were factory workers—there was no uniform process of job decline. Instead, work histories showed a shift from reliance on work to reliance on family or welfare. For the 1900s cohort cross-tabulation of principal occupation by present occupation produces a correlation (gamma) of 0.81, indicating extreme stability. By 1940 the gamma was 0.27; the drop in the correlation was not due to movement from one occupational category to a lesser one, but rather to the movement from principal occupation to "none"—that is, to reliance on public welfare.

The stability of the 1900s cohort masks some underemployment: an important minority of the men experienced severe job decline *within* their regular profession, taking less and less prestigious positions. Oscar Carver is a case in point: after a start as a clerk in an insurance company, Carver rose to become a member of the firm; the company failed; and Carver found work as a clerk in a smaller firm until forced by ill health to stop.[22] The general picture, however, is one of job continuity. By the 1940s an entirely different scenario had emerged: 91 percent of the men reported no present occupation (under "means of support," only 2 percent reported work). Men no longer continued to work or *planned* to work at their trade in their old age.

Again, no evidence exists of job decline among these 1940s cases. Men simply stopped working within their principal occupation—because of injury, illness, failure of the firm, being discharged—and Old Age Assistance or Social Security supported them. The 1940s cohort shows the profound effects of state relief: men did not continue to work in their

Table IV–3.
Means of Support of HAM Clients by Cohort

Means of Support	1900s (%)	1920s (%)	1940s (%)
Work	27	21	2
Savings	8	7	3
Pension[a]	2	7	16
Relatives, Friends	8	21	3
Public Relief	0	14	56
Other Relief[b]	12	24	8
None	44	7	13
	(n = 52)	(n = 29)	(n = 63)

NOTE: Missing data: 3 cases for 1900s, 5 for 1920s, 12 for 1940s; rounding errors cause deviations from 100 percent in totals for columns.

[a] Includes Social Security (Old Age Insurance) in 1940s.

[b] Includes private relief, private and public relief, and work and relief.

old age; they did not find less and less prestigious positions within their chief occupations; nor did they fall into a different job category. The overwhelming majority of the men dropped out of work altogether.

How did they survive? Responses of applicants when asked their means of support provide a fuller understanding of the changing occupational circumstances of older men. "Means of support," a subject dear to the inquisitorial hearts of the Home's admitting committees and social workers, can be broken down into several broad categories (Table IV-3). It can be seen that in the earliest period older men relied on income from work or savings (both often meager); if these failed, they had few other resources. The largest group claimed no means of support; as we have seen, many of the HAM clients depended on their principal vocation for survival and, losing that, applied for aid.

Across the century, work became less central as a means of support, and particularly so in the 1940s cohort. The most consistent upward trend is in relief. If we combine public and private sources, the percentages of men receiving relief at the time of their application to the HAM rose from 12 to 38 to 64. By the 1940s public Old Age Assistance was supporting more than half the men who applied, and work, savings, and relatives/friends disappeared as means of support. Old men had "gone on the Old Age." If we include pensions (largely Social Security insurance), public funds reached about two-thirds of all applicants. This enormous expansion is responsible for the contrast between the choices and circumstances of old age before and after the New Deal.

Occupational data from HAW case records on the male relatives of the indigent women parallel HAM records, but, as Chapter III made clear, the working lives of women are dramatically different. First, it is clear that, like the HAM, the HAW never served a once prestigious group that had fallen on hard times. In a random survey of occupations among 29 clients in the 1850s, 12 of the women reported domestic employment, 5 were nurses, and 7 were seamstresses. Of 18 fathers' occupations recorded, 1 was LBC, 3 were farmers, 11 were SBC, and 3 were from white-collar backgrounds. This is a group not of ladies, but of women whose husbands and fathers held blue-collar jobs and whose own occupations provided little security for old age. The pattern continued across the remainder of the nineteenth century: of 24 cases selected randomly from records between 1861 and 1890, 17 of the women had LBC occupations; the majority of fathers and husbands had been SBC workers.[23]

The HAW retained its working-class constituency in the twentieth century. SBC occupations predominated among the women's spouses, accounting for 52 percent, with LWC jobs second, at 30 percent. Of the women themselves the great majority listed one of four occupations—housewife (recorded as "none"), domestic servant, nurse, or seamstress—I have placed all seamstresses in the LBC category, along with domestics. Nurses received SBC classification,

Table IV–4.
Principal Occupation of HAW Clients by Cohort and
Demicentury

	Cohorts			
Occupation	1900s (%)	1920s (%)	1940s (%)	1900–1950 (%)
None	10	8	26	17
LBC	63	44	22	42
SBC	6	22	20	15
LWC	21	25	29	25
MWC	0	0	4	2
	(n = 67)	(n = 36)	(n = 77)	(n = 180)

NOTE: Rounding errors cause deviations from 100 percent in totals for columns.

surely exaggerating the level of skill involved in nursing at this time.[24]

Table IV-4 shows the occupational distribution of the clients of the charity by cohorts and for the demicentury. Comparison with the data secured from the HAW's brother institution reveals the much greater significance of LBC occupations among the women than among HAM clients (42 versus 13 percent).

The old women left sound testimony to their "laborious and useful occupations;"[25] their records relate a grim account of toil, quite in keeping with the opportunities available to women in the American labor market as reviewed in Chapter III. The conclusion is plain: if the HAM was a clerk's home, the HAW was, in 1900, the domestic servant's last refuge. The SBC category, into which practical nurses were placed, includes many women whose work was really a form of domestic service. In sum, this most respectable of charitable homes was filled with housekeepers, laundresses, charwomen, and attendants.

One can read the work experience of these relatively advantaged Yankee women as an account of their degradation. But how does the tabulation in Table IV-4 correspond with the discussion of women's work in Chapter III? A comparison may be summarized in three major points:

1. The HAW women worked, which makes them different from most women. Although the data are not perfectly comparable, it is clear that these women had much more extensive work experience, and more experience in their later years, than the average aged Boston woman.
2. We know that almost no older women could be found in LWC occupations in 1900, and there were few in 1920. The women from the HAW, despite the large numbers in LBC work, had extraordinarily high concentrations of white-collar workers. These Yankee women were privileged in comparison to most of their aged sisters in the Boston labor force.
3. The cohort effect is visible in the work records of the HAW. The decline in LBC work reflects the fact that the last cohorts of *native* women working in domestic service were an aging group at the turn of the century. After this period few native-born women entered domestic service. Some older women, especially widows, remained in this category using ill-rewarded domestic skills, and their fate is discussed below. But, as Yankees, HAW women escaped some of the worst effects of the twentieth-century labor market for women

A review of the cohorts in Table IV-4 shows the gradual upgrading of occupational status during the first 50 years of the century. That 21 percent of the 1900s cohort had achieved white-collar status—securing their positions during the nineteenth century—is testimony to the advantages that these Yankee women enjoyed; as late as 1910 less than 20 percent of the female labor force were white-collar workers, and much less of the aged female labor force.[26] Nevertheless, as we have seen, the largest category remained LBC into the 1920s cohort. These data confirm the findings in Chapter III: the heralded expansion of the female clerical work force at the turn of the century worked its initial effects on *young* women. MWC employment remained closed even to these Yankees, paragons of respectability. Instead women parlayed what they learned at the hearth: the domestic skills of sewing, cleaning, cooking, and nursing. These were among the most poorly paid of all talents.[27] Domestic work accounted for about one-fourth of all women workers 65 and over in Boston in 1890; laboring at jobs increasingly filled by immigrant women, aged Yankee women showed the customary occupational "backwardness" of older cohorts observed in Chapter III. The records of the HAW show that women were compelled to accept one of a limited and unattractive group of alternatives: to labor as a servant in another person's home, to do piece work (primarily sewing) at home, or to pursue light factory work, especially sewing in the shops in the garment district, mixing with immigrant women in an unpleasant and unremunerative approximation of factory life. The history of these older women, and the ambiguity of the transition from the hearth to the factory, resound in a comment by an aged woman (not connected to the HAW) who worked in Boston's garment district: "I did sewing. I mean I was a dressmaker. I mean I worked in a factory."[28]

A plain affinity obtained between women's work inside and outside the home. If she was without husband, without family, she earned her keep at some of society's most arduous and unrewarding tasks: cleaning, cooking, sewing, tending the sick. If she had a husband and family, she performed precisely the same duties. Indeed, the division between paid and unpaid female labor is an artificial one; the rise of feminist scholarship has brought back the old socialist argument that housework *is* work.[29]

Perhaps the only advantage in this line of work was that it could be continued in old age. But continued at great cost—age was a ferocious combatant. Carrie Burnham found herself, in her sixties, "sewing at starvation prices" in a belt factory; she remarked that often she could not "get on my boots my feet are so swollen." The nurses who approached the Home for assistance saw age as a great liability: Eva Webster noted that there was little "employment [given] to nurses passed 60 years," and Alice Piper, at 69, saw her own future: "I get very tired and it is to be expected that I'll not be able to continue work much longer."[30]

Only one other alternative existed for these women, and its growth can be seen in the expansion in the percentage of women who had never held a job: from 10 percent in the 1900s to 26 percent in the 1940s. The sudden increase in the 1940s follows directly from the nature of government welfare; neither Old Age Assistance nor Social Security survivor's benefits required a work history for qualification and housewives could apply.

Nonetheless, many older women worked to support themselves in old age, and, in fact, the percentage of applicants reporting work as a means of support rose from 25 percent to 34 percent between 1900 and 1950. These women relied on work because they could not rely on a husband's wages; most had no man to call on. Of all clients, 38 percent were single, and 53 percent were widows. Widows had on average lost their husbands 20 years before application and inherited minimal savings or resources: 69 percent reported that their husbands left them nothing.[31] Mrs. Clementine Wales was able to live on her husband's property until her sixties. Then she found herself forced to work first as a seamstress in a rug works and, when she lost that job, as a laundress. Lacking the strength to do washing, she returned to sewing: "at 72 years of age, I find myself unable to compete with the younger persons who do the sewing and sometimes [I] have little to eat." Mrs. Dora Dearing was left a widow at 33 with three children; 80 at the time of application, she entreated the Admissions Committee not to deny her because she was old and feeble: "Brought up my children without any help never weighed 100 lb. Do you think I have worked years enough."[32] These woeful stories did not issue from women whose husbands were utter failures. More than half of the husbands had been SBC workers, and 40 percent had been white-collar employees. But, as seen in the occupational histories collected by the HAM, the SBC and LWC backgrounds of their husbands hardly guaranteed security in old age for self or spouse. Nor was the problem that the married couples had squandered their funds providing for children; rather the reverse, as we shall see: they had failed to procreate enough sons and daughters to ensure support in old age. In addition, widowhood carried a special penalty in that the female labor market reserved its greatest terrors for those women compelled to enter it late in life. This condition has been discussed in Chapter III, using aggregate data. It appears even more clearly in these detailed individual histories. Crosstabulation of principal occupation with marital status among HAW women tells volumes about the effects of marriage on occupational experience. A few widows—especially after the institution of social security—enjoyed the luxury of being adequately provided for; of the 30 clients who reported never having held an occupation outside the home, 26 were widows. But these relatively fortunate women made up less than one-third of the widowed group. Of the 70 widows who had to go out to work, almost 75 percent ended up in LBC occupations. Single women, on the other hand, 38 percent of clients as a whole, constituted only 3 percent of those who had never worked. Obviously single women suffered one penalty as a result of their marital status: they had to work. But they commanded great advantages in the labor market. Thirty-eight percent of all single women were in LWC occupations, as opposed to 17 percent of the widows. These comparisons reveal a significant difference in experience based on marital status. Single women worked most of their lives, and under that necessity were more likely to prepare themselves for a career and to have more years to climb such job ladders as existed for women. In addition, they were able to gain entry into new employment areas for women in their youth, while married women practiced the traditional household skills that later translated into LBC work.[33] Living on a deceased husband's savings was not a reasonable alternative for HAW women, whose average age at the time of the husband's death was 51. Their skills, and the chronic shortage of servants,[34] pointed the way for widows: among 26 who reported that they had never held a principal occupation (most widowed late in life), 9 had just taken up work, all but one in a LBC occupation. The experience was not a pleasant one, as Emma Webster reported: "Have disposed of all jewelry ornaments and clothing by piece . . . to get money to live on."[35]

The study of HAW clients reveals an important minority group among working women at the beginning of the century: widows bound into the lowest occupational categories. Widows and a much smaller number of divorced women constituted about 15 percent of the female labor force in 1890, and constitute (with a larger proportion of divorced women) about 20 percent in recent years.[36] The drama of the recent movement of married women into the labor force has obscured the striking resemblances between these newcomers and early twentieth-century widows. The current (but flattening) double-peaked curve in female LFPR (high in the early twenties, sharply declining in the childbearing years, and high again in the 40–55 age group) was foreshadowed in the early part of the century by the gradual return of widowed women to the labor force. In fact, a cohort born between 1876 and 1885 peaked in participation at ages 14–24 and then began a steady decline until ages 45–54 (in 1930), when participation increased, as in recent times; in the earlier case, however, the rise in labor force activity occurred because of a higher incidence of widowhood.[37]

In qualitative if not quantitative terms, the widow of the

past and the married working woman of the 1980s are similar: they are middle-aged, and they enter the labor market relatively untrained and without work experience since their early twenties. It could be argued that another similarity obtains between these historical groups. Women worked then and work now in a secondary labor market, characterized by marginal businesses, low wages, part-time employment, high turnover, and minimal advancement.[38] In the early twentieth century, HAW records show the particular proclivity of widows for jobs in this sector. Debate continues over whether labor market segmentation results from deliberately discriminatory practices at the firm level. Those who criticize the claim that women are consciously discriminated against point to older women's lower human capital, discontinuous work histories, and lower returns to training as legitimate reasons for their segregation in inferior occupational sectors.[39] Certainly the widows of the HAW brought poor credentials when they applied for a job. They had little investment in the market training conducive to success. One father, "believing that he would always be able to take care of his daughters[,] did not train them to any useful occupation."[40] Ill-prepared to enter the paid labor force, these women fared poorly in it.

These case records offer no empirical grounds for a test of the question of discrimination, although a historian finds it difficult to believe that the hiring officer of the nineteenth-century firm did not practice at work what he surely preached at home. But manifest evidence exists that the sexual division of labor—the sexist preparation that everyone agrees reduces women's occupational success—had profound implications for women's work lives and hence, as these dismal records show, for the quality of their lives. For the women *did* get training; there was investment in their human capital: they learned to clean, sew, cook, and attend to children and the sick. Nor was their work career discontinuous—it was monotonously continuous. But the training, the career, the skills, developed were those of the wife, and cheaply bought at that.

This comparison of the widow of the 1920s and the married woman of the 1980s has left out the single most important difference. However discriminatory the market may be, however low the pay and attenuated the opportunities, contemporary married women usually work to *supplement* family income. Granting exceptions to this rule and the right of women today to good jobs and pay, the distance from the widow of the early twentieth century is striking: she worked to eat.

The records of the HAW between 1900 and 1950 paint a dark picture of the older working woman in this period. Such women, especially widows, had to work in a labor market notable for its deficiency of opportunity. The chief occupational category—LBC—comprised jobs whose main virtues were that they were "naturally" suited to women's skills and that they could be retained in old age. A bleak work life followed directly from the training in nonmarket activities guaranteed these women because of their sex. Schooled in family chores, their chief liability was lack of a family in which to work.

The Family of
the Dependent Aged

The dissimilarity of work experience between male and female clients in the charitable homes followed from the nature of the female labor market. But both sexes ended their lives in overt dependency, only their ethnicity saving them from complete disgrace in the city almshouse. Their varying occupational histories do not predict their dependency well. If anything, these men and women exceeded their non-Yankee counterparts in access to good jobs. The deficiency that threw them into the arms of charity in old age was lack of family. The role of the family as the basic welfare institution in American society and its persistence as a source of support for older Bostonians were explored in Chapter II. The welfare responsibilities of family members were closely prescribed in the early twentieth century, and the HAM and HAW followed the conventional belief—embodied in the statutes of Massachusetts in 1915[41]—that no aged person should be given aid who could be supported by his or her family.

Christine McLeod, social worker for the HAM from 1921 to 1939, took great pains to ensure that no member of the family—immediate or remote—escaped scrutiny as a possible source of support for an aged relative. Admitting committees were determined that families should assist their aged members, and each applicant was carefully questioned about spouse, children, siblings, and other family members.[42]

Most of the HAM clients could not rely on wives for support in their old age. Across the period from 1900 to 1950, 62 percent were either single or widowed; only in the 1940s did married men become a large part of those aided. The case records convey a sense of both financial and personal helplessness on the part of recent widowers; the HAM became the wife who supports the aging husband.

No fact emerges more starkly from the case records of the HAM than the deficiency of family structure among those who sought aid. After his wife, children were the most likely source of assistance for a man unable to support himself. Yet, as Table IV-5 shows, men aided by the HAM did not have this resource. Fathers had often lost contact with children, as Paul Banks lamented in the early twentieth century: "I am unaware if my two children are alive or dead." Charles Bartlett reported himself the "last of my name and family."[43] Single men and men with no surviving children made up over half of the old men aided; this constituted the population that the HAM was most likely to assist.

These family deficiencies extended to other relatives as

Table IV–5.
HAW and HAM Clients by Number of Children, 1900–1950

Number of Children	HAW (%)	HAM (%)
(Single)	(39)	(21)
0	39	34
1	15	19
2	2	12
3 or More	5	14
Total	100	100
	(n = 176)	(n = 160)

NOTE: Four cases in each sample were missing data. Among HAW clients, the mean number of children was 0.37; if one excludes single women, it was 0.60. For the HAM, the mean number of children equalled 0.91; if one excludes bachelors, 1.15.

well. Many men listed relatives as living in other states or as unheard from in many years. John Hepworth remarked that he had a "millionaire uncle out west" but felt that he could not count on him.[44] A reasonable measure of the *effective* kinship network available to these men is the number of relatives of any kind, including children, living in Massachusetts. By this measure the abbreviation of the family group of HAM clients was extreme in comparison with the ordinary family circumstances of the aged as described in Chapter II. The mean number of such relatives was 1.4, and 30 percent of the men reported no relatives in Massachusetts.[45] This small network of kin, which includes relatives neither willing, able, nor legally obliged to support the aged men, demonstrates the inadequacy of the family as a support mechanism for the clients of the HAM.

A still more striking familial isolation marks the women of the HAW, even with generous discounting for fraudulent application. The women had even fewer children and relatives than the quite bereft men of the HAM, as Table IV-5 reveals. They were, as one applicant said of herself, "lonely," and it is isolation that explains their public dependency.[46] They had remained single, or their marriages had been broken by death. These two categories account for 91 percent of HAW clients. (Data for all of Boston's aged women, presented in Chapter II, indicate that 70 to 75 percent were single or widowed.) Add to these a few separated and divorced women, and the percentage of women unattached to men stood in the 1900s at 96 percent, in the 1920s at 92 percent, and in the 1940s at 100 percent.[47] As our review of their occupations has illustrated, the early loss of husband was not propitious. In addition, marriage had not provided these women with the primary bulwark against overt dependency in old age: numerous children. Single women and women with no surviving children made up more than 77 percent of those who applied to the HAW. (Among ever-married women the number of children averaged 0.6.)

Denied the possibility of support from children, the women could not have turned to other relatives. The number of Massachusetts relatives averaged about one per client, with 40 percent claiming no relative in the state. Thus, the women had no effective kinship network. The HAW served a specific population that was at risk: old women, single or widowed, who had no family to turn to.

The family pattern observed changed little over time. Put in the most general terms, the women and men who appealed to these Homes were isolates, lacking an effective family group when their occupational support failed them. The case records reveal what the aggregate census data showed previously: the historical continuity of the family as the center of well-being for the aged, and most especially for women who could find little recourse in work. Peter Townsend's conclusions about the institutionalized aged in England and the 1960s could be applied to the clients of the HAW and HAM: "What stands out . . . is the absence of practicable alternatives, of supporting relatives, friends, and social services."[48]

Conclusions

What conclusions may be drawn from the HAM and HAW evidence? First, the officers' critical view of the effects of relief on character and their ethnocentric bias strained the quality of mercy. Founded by welfare reformers who sought to restrict almsgiving, and, in the twentieth century, wedded to a powerful Protestant welfare establishment still committed to this principle, the two institutions resisted generous public *or* private benevolence. They shared ethnocentric biases with most of Boston's private charities; old age charitable organizations generally limited assistance to specific religious, ethnic, or racial groups, and the powerful central agencies, such as the Boston Provident Association, displayed a distinctly Protestant ethos. Catholics, denied access to certain Boston charities and loath to accept aid from many of the rest, had claim to an archdiocesan system more generous in spirit but poorer in pocket. In summary, the private charity system limited relief in general, then further limited it to certain deserving groups.

For those of British ethnicity and Protestant convictions, the HAM and HAW provided help. Such elderly were not a majority in Boston's aged population, nor the group most likely to need assistance, but the dependent among them had a special appeal. Advocates of new welfare programs argued that modern conditions made the middle classes vulnerable to poverty in old age. Although the HAM and HAW clients were not middle class, they displayed highly "respectable" working-class and LWC backgrounds, with enviable records of sobriety and good moral conduct. Still, they ended as paupers—lucky paupers in that they were Yankees, but paupers nonetheless.

Before the 1940s the men relied for their support on work, generally in their principal occupations, until ill health or other calamity forced them to the HAM. Only a minority fell into lesser occupations or poorer grades within a principal calling; for the majority, the termination of principal occupation commenced the period of dependency. The women told a grimmer occupational tale. Although a minority rose above their non-Yankee sisters by securing white-collar employment, most suffered the double jeopardy of being old and female. Ill-fitted for a female labor market already narrowly defined, the aged clients of the HAW found themselves forced to seek work in the LBC occupations for which "female" skills prepared them. The LBC labor market welcomed older women; and it paid neither wages nor benefits sufficient to support retirement in old age. Of all women, widows qualified best for the worst employment. Their husbands' occupations did not provide security for a 30-year widowhood, and married life gave them just those skills least valued in the labor market.

The chief finding in these records, however, is that the occupational records of the clients are secondary in explaining old age dependency. Family network, not occupation, predicts overt dependency. If illness or widowhood or other misfortune severed an aged person from the income of a principal occupation, as it did for large number of Boston's elders, overt dependency did not necessarily follow. But if this misfortune was accompanied by isolation from a family network, the older person had to beg openly for charity.

The obvious nature of their overt dependency obscures something of still broader importance. Older people with neither an occupation nor an effective family network were a very small minority of the aged population of Boston. A much larger group, made up primarily of old women, had no occupational resources, but did have a family upon which to rely. It is this *covert* dependency on family that the unusual overt dependency of the HAM and HAW reveals.

For every old person forced to ask for public or private relief, many more relied on adult children or other relatives for food, lodging, and nursing care. The social workers of the private charities tried to press family members to assist, and they lamented the decline of family feeling when adult children failed to support their aged parents. They opposed state relief, partly because it threatened their careers, but also because they perceived that state welfare would replace family obligations, further eroding the one institution that could give to the poor without corrupting them.[49]

The hidden structure of old age dependency marks especially the history of older women. Older men usually commanded respect and wages in the labor market in the early twentieth century. But before the rise of public welfare, the older woman had no reasonable alternative to reliance on husband and family. Her labors—onerous, poorly paid, and vacant of security—provided but a temporary solution. The widow's unenviable lot was to be *compelled* to seek help from children or relatives. Historians of the family have recently advanced two theories, each of which obfuscates the widow's historical experience. One theory celebrates the resiliency and supportiveness of the family as a welfare mechanism; the other, in opposition, raises the traditional lament of the decline of the family as bureaucratic social welfare services replace its functions.[50] Both ignore a not inconsiderable body of women who had no family to turn to. More important, both ignore the malign consequences of dependency *within* the family. We cannot imagine that all old women or men found it comforting to be received into their children's homes as charity cases, to work if the children demanded it, and to have no reasonable alternative.

In his brief historical study of family relationships and governmental welfare for the aged in England, Michael Anderson argues that "both in the prepension and postpension period the majority of the institutionalized population are not living in the community either because they need intensive medical attention or because they have no relatives to help them." Before pensions, however, support within the family had enormous costs, for "the obligation to assist was often a source of tension between parents and children throughout the nineteenth century"; the old were often compelled to coreside with children and other relatives, without a pension to sweeten their way, despite the disharmony this might create—disharmony for which Anderson offers chilling evidence.[51]

Social security freed old age relief from its ethnocentrism and from the implication that assistance corrupted the recipient. It gave men and women a measure of security that occupations could never supply. And it released older people who could not hold a job from utter dependence on family or charity, sanctuaries perhaps less benevolent and receptive than they appear. The origins of the social security solution lie in the public welfare system, where ethnic, working-class constituencies sought to use their political power to expand relief and eliminate the biases that pervaded private charity, to end the insecurity that accompanied all but the highest occupations, and, perhaps most important, to relieve the hidden pressure—on aged people and the family alike—of covert dependency.

Chapter V
Public Welfare: The Boston Almshouse

Had the Brahmins had their way, public welfare would have been limited to the poorhouse—an ideal device to reduce appeals for assistance. For the most unfortunate of Boston's aged, poverty and lack of family led to commitment to the city's pauper institutions. These almshouses differed from the private homes first in the clientele they served. Ethnic, working-class elders filled Boston's almshouses. Between 1900 and 1950 the almshouse population closely reflected the changing ethnic character of Boston's aged population. The inmates' LBC occupational histories had set up minimal defenses against misfortune in old age. The Irish Catholic domestic who had labored in Yankee houses for 30 years got her reward in old age at the poorhouse, not at the HAW. But her gravest liability was not religion or occupation, but a failing shared with her worthy Protestant sisters. For almshouse inmates suffered from the same weakness as the "better" class of pauper found in the private homes: they too had no families. A limited family network, for the Irish hod carrier as well as the Yankee clerk, emerges as the *sine qua non* of institutionalization.

Although the institutionalized Yankees and Irish shared a vulnerability based on insufficient family resources, their punishments differed sharply. The public almshouse, once the center of a punitive welfare system for all ages, retained

128

its noxious and degrading character even as it was transformed into a public old age home. To be "sent down the Island," as Bostonians referred to incarceration at the institution in the city's bay, was to end up wrecked and ruined in the harbor that many of the immigrants had so hopefully sailed through 50 years before. As American poorhouses filled with old people, critics came to describe the public institutions as "concentration camps for the aged"; and the consignment of the elderly to almshouses supplied the movement for state old age relief with its most poignant symbol.[1]

For the frailest and most isolated of the non-Yankee aged, dependency meant incarceration at the principal city poorhouse, a large facility on Long Island, five miles from Boston. Most of the urban elders who boarded the city steamer for Long Island ended their lives there. In this chapter, their almshouse experience is described first through the general institutional records, an approach that captures one part of the nature of commitment to a poorhouse in old age. But samples of the case records of the inmates provided a much fuller picture of life in the house. The ethnic, occupational, and familial characteristics of these old people lead directly to the central issues in the debate over old age dependency in the early twentieth century.

To Long Island

On cool fall afternoons welfare agents brought the old people, most of them old women in wheelchairs or on cots, to the Eastern Avenue Wharf.[2] The steamer *George Bradlee*, leaking city money, awaited them, displaying on its prow pole the blue banner of the Institutions Department. Across the gangplank the nurses and attendants shepherded the grayhaired, sick, dipsomaniac, and feeble out of Boston and into the harbor waters. Past Castle Island, Thompson's, and the smoking, stinking garbage of Spectacle Island, the *Bradlee* steamed and coughed until its passengers' small rooms and few relatives lay five miles behind. The great wooden wharf of Long Island Almshouse and Hospital greeted them. Along the Island's crest stood a motley collection of buildings, some constructed in the grandiose manner of the nineteenth-century institutional architect, some jerrybuilt in the timeless budget-conscious style.

In the sharp wind, the first medical officer met the elders, whom he consigned to hospital or dormitory. Self-interest led him to assign many to the hospital for "treatment," although most would receive only nursing and custodial care.[3] The physician also determined which ward they would be assigned to—phthisis, senile, venereal—if the hospital had room at the time for classification and segregation. Head nurses met patients at the receiving room of the wards, a house officer determined what treatment they would receive, and, if well enough, the patients were assigned ward work.

Medical officers soon transferred most old people to the dormitory (the custodial or nursing section), where they spent the greater part of the remainder of their lives. Here attendants supplied each of them with institutional clothing, a bed, and a place at table and assigned the few old men and women capable of any labor to various tasks around the Island. House officers could impose solitary confinement in the "jail" on the able-bodied who refused to work. The majority of the elderly did not work but, in good weather, passed their time sitting on the porches, looking across the bare fields to the sea that they had once crossed with some anticipation, and watching the cats work the refuse barrels outside the fetid morgue.

In places such as these a small percentage of the American elderly lived. Visited by periodic scandal, characterized by routine corruption and noxious conditions, the public almshouse had never achieved the ambitious goals of its antebellum founders, who thought it would deter mendicants and reduce relief taxes. By the turn of the century, the American poorhouse more and more resembled a public old age home. Stripped of the punitive functions intended by its nineteenth century creators and deprived of younger clients by new institutions for special categories of dependency, the American almshouse became a custodial nursing facility for the old.[4] The Long Island Almshouse of the city of Boston typified the evolution toward a public old age home. In the late nineteenth century, the city had periodically reorganized its pauper and criminal institutions, searching (vainly) for a happy combination of classification and economy. In the 1890s the city built a large island almshouse and attached to it a pauper hospital. The Long Island facilities accounted for one-sixth of all the almshouse inmates in Massachusetts and consumed a considerable proportion of city welfare expenditures.[5]

Although Massachusetts law stipulated that the public almshouse must furnish a place of last resort for all poor, indigent, or incapacitated people without relatives liable for their support, its actual clientele varied as the definition of accepted public social welfare functions changed. Despite repeated criticisms of the practice of mixing the worthy poor with the "vicious" or mildly criminal type, Boston often sent alcoholics and petty criminals to Long Island.[6] In this and other respects the Long Island Almshouse displayed an ambiguity of purpose. On the one hand, economy, theory, and tradition supported a punitive house of detention for all those incapable of or resistant to work, a forbidding institution designed to warn the nonproductive, and provide a last resort against outright starvation. On the other hand, it was clear to many observers at the turn of the century that the almshouse was becoming something quite different: specifically, a long-term nursing home for old people with varying degrees of incapacity, joined by a temporary population of men and women incapacitated by drink, injury, or illness. By the late nineteenth century, American almshouses were filling up with the feeble aged. Their function as punitive

Table V–1.
United States Almshouse Population by Age Group, 1880–1923

Age Group	1880 (%)	1904 (%)	1923 (%)
35–44	14	10	6
65 and Over	26	41	54

SOURCES: U.S. Department of Commerce, Bureau of the Census, *Paupers in Almshouses: 1910* (Washington, D.C., 1915), pp. 17, 89; *Paupers in Almshouses: 1923* (Washington, D.C., 1925), p. 10.
NOTE: Almshouse residents were enumerated on a single day in each year.

relief institutions for some categories of the poor continued as the perennial schemes for separating poorhouses from correctional facilities died for want of money. Nonetheless, the growth of institutional and noninstitutional alternatives for children, mothers with dependent children, the insane, the sick, and the mentally retarded meant that the almshouse served a primary population of aged people and a secondary and transient population of the mildly deviant.[7]

Boston followed this national pattern. Thus, the population likely to be confined in almshouses shifted from middle-aged, highly employable people to older age groups (see Table V-1). In 1880 men and women 65 and over made up about one-quarter of the national almshouse populations; in 1923, over half. Less detailed statistics for Massachusetts show that in 1890 those 35 to 44 composed 12 percent of the almshouse population, while those 65 and over made up 36 percent. In 1923 the corresponding percentages were 5 and 48. During the 1880s, Boston almshouse officers had noted the shift in the age distribution of inmates.[8]

This transformation had important effects, but these should not be misread. As W. Andrew Achenbaum has argued, the shift toward an older clientele did not mean that an old person's risk of entering the almshouse had increased, since the proportion of the elderly in the population rose during the same time period. In fact, while the risk of confinement in the poorhouse declined rapidly for the population as a whole, it remained constant for the aged. Between 1880 and 1923 the proportion of the U.S. population living in almshouses fell from 1.3 to 0.74 persons in every 1,000. Among highly employable middle-aged groups (aged 35–44) the almshouse threat faded even more, from 1.7 to 0.34 persons per 1,000. For the aged, however, the risk neither increased nor declined. In 1880 about 10 in every 1,000 persons 65 and over lived in almshouses; in 1923, about 9. Younger people probably lost the traditional dread of the house—a dread nurtured by elites over the previous century—but for the aged the adage that one should face the world with "a reverence for God, the hope of heaven, and the fear of the poorhouse" was neither more nor less true. The transformation of the almshouse into an old age home only kept pace with the rapid expansion of the aged population, and therefore almshouse data alone indicate no increasing overt dependency among the aged.[9]

Nonetheless, the spectable of run-down poorhouses now filled with decrepit old people and alcoholics had powerful symbolic effect, and the consignment of the aged to the poorhouse was loudly attacked by the Fraternal Order of Eagles and other groups pressing for state old age relief programs.[10] Boston almshouses received similar criticism because they shared in the trend toward the segregation of the dependent aged in institutions designed for the undeserving and therefore deliberately degrading to the inmate. City officials recognized that the elderly were often considered to be among the "worthy" poor and made attempts to shield them from the worst institutional conditions.

In 1898 the city set aside one of its institutions as the "Almshouse for Women and Aged Couples," a decaying building said to have "more the appearance of an old women's home than a public institution."[11] About a hundred inmates lived there. At first most were women, but by the time of its abandonment half were men. The Charlestown superintendent claimed that this almshouse aided the "worthy poor," whereas Long Island had to serve the "poor of all classes."[12] Public officials shared with private welfare leaders the belief that paupers of the "better and worthy class" were subject to "pain . . . by immediate association with rough and vulgar" types and therefore deserved separate quarters.[13] However, the special almshouse, the city's concession to this brand of thinking and to the general uneasiness about the practice of housing old people with the deviant, was not large enough to permit complete separation and was abandoned in 1915.[14]

Certainly the city's welfare officers faced a growing challenge in the proportion of aged among persons admitted to the almshouses. The transformation of the almshouse quickly became evident; in the early twentieth century, city officials recognized that there had been a substantial "increase of the aged and feeble element of the population."[15] The trustees of the city's pauper institutions commented in 1899: "Any one visiting the island at most seasons of the year [excepting winter] must be struck with the fact that the aged and infirm predominate."[16] Between 1904 and 1917 the proportion aged 55 and over among those admitted rose from 31 percent to 44 percent (Table V-2). Admission records actually obscure the aging of the almshouse population, since younger persons tended to be transient and older ones permanent inmates. City reports rarely provided the age distribution of the actual population in the almshouse at one time. In one of the few reports analyzing the population by age on a given day (31 January 1905), the predominance of the aged is more clearly shown (Table V-3). Even at this relatively early date, men 55 and over constituted 37 percent of the male inmate population and women of the same age fully 70 percent of their gender. The percentages of aged shown in Table V-3, while substantially higher than the corresponding figures for admission records, remain decep-

Table V–2.

Boston Almshouse Admissions by Age Group, 1905–1917

	Year Ending 31 January			
Age Group	1905 (%)	1909 (%)	1913 (%)	1917 (%)
16–35	22	18	15	14
35–55	47	45	44	42
55–65	17 ⎫	21 ⎫	23 ⎫	25 ⎫
65–75	10 ⎬ 31	11 ⎬ 37	13 ⎬ 40	15 ⎬ 44
75 and Over	4 ⎭	5 ⎭	4 ⎭	4 ⎭
	(n = 1,053)	(n = 1,116)	(n = 1,157)	(n = 937)

SOURCES: "Annual Report of the Pauper Institutions Department," *Documents of the City of Boston, 1905*, vol. 2, no. 29, pp. 29–30 (hereafter *DCB*); "Twelfth Annual Report for the Boston Infirmary Department," *DCB, 1909*, vol. 2, no. 28, pp. 34–35; "Sixteenth Annual Report of the Boston Infirmary Department" *DCB, 1913*, vol. 2, no. 17, pp. 36–37 (hereafter "ARBID"); "Twentieth ARBID," *DCB, 1917*, vol. 1, no. 5, pp. 31–32.

NOTE: The repetition of a year (e.g., 16–35 and 35–55), an error in the original records, could not be corrected. Rounding errors cause deviations in 100 percent in totals for columns.

Table V–3.

Boston Almshouse Inmates on 31 January 1905 by Age and Sex

Age Group	Men (%)	Women (%)	Total (%)
16–35	11	8	10
35–55	52	22	39
55–65	18	28	23
65–75	13	28	19
75 and Over	6	14	10
	(n = 637)	(n = 476)	(n = 1,113)

SOURCE: "Annual Report of the Pauper Institutions Department," *DCB 1905*, vol. 2, no. 29, pp. 32–33.

NOTE: Rounding errors cause deviations in 100 percent in totals for columns.

tively low, since the temporary deviant (alcoholic) population—consisting mostly of younger men—reached its height at about this time of year. In sum, at least one-half of the daily population in the almshouse was 55 and over, and one-third was 65 and over. One-half of the female inmate population was 65 and over. Using these figures, we can estimate that the Boston almshouses incarcerated about 1.5 percent of the city's aged population (65 and over) in 1905. This estimate corresponds with Massachusetts levels and exceeds national percentages.[17]

The Long Island population differs most strikingly from national almshouse populations in the very large number of aged women. In the 1905 census there were about 200 women 65 and over to about 125 men. In part the female predominance reflects the fact that Boston's aged population was predominately female, a demographic condition found in Chapter II to characterize a number of large metropolitan areas.

Nonetheless, most almshouse populations were overwhelmingly male. In 1910, in both the United States as a whole and New England, where poorhouses were extensively used, women had much lower incarceration rates. Even in the older age groups, almsmen outnumbered almswomen by two to one. For the United States in 1923, among those inmates aged 80 to 84, there were 35 men to every 20 women. It is said that gender differences in almshouse commitment follow from a tradition that women should not be sent to the almshouse, a sentiment expressed by Boston's relief officers in the early twentieth century. Contemporary observation, as well as recent research, suggests that women could get outdoor relief (i.e., aid in their own residences) more readily, could handle household duties alone more effectively, and, if needy, were more welcome in the homes of their children.[18]

These resources were not sufficient for Boston's aged women. Examination of Boston's public welfare system confirms the tendency of welfare officials to give outdoor relief to aged women, and private charity provided more resources for women than men. The particular vulnerability of Boston almswomen lay, as we shall see, in the breakdown of the last resource—the availability of family for support.

For such information we cannot rely on regular institutional records. Although the published records of the Long Island Almshouse reveal its general character and confirm its transformation into the city old age home, the inmates themselves remain inaccessible in such documents. Who were these poorhouse folk, Sarah Orne Jewett's "creatures of improvidence and misfortune, and the irreparable victims of old age"?[19] For each of his passengers, the mate of the *Bradlee* received an investigation blank on which were recorded bits of the old person's history, the names of relatives and friends, birthplace, and religion. From these data we can piece together a more precise picture of the unfortunates who sailed out from Boston to end their lives on Long Island.

The Inmates

Almshouse officials used the investigation blanks to begin a case record for each admission to Long Island. These records, regularly updated during the inmate's confinement, reveal the route to dependency and the course of the elder's almshouse life. Approximately 6,600 case records remain of persons 60 and over admitted to the facility between 1900 and 1950. Simple random samples of three categories of clients were taken from these records: (1) males 60 and over who died at Long Island (n = 343); (2) females 60 and over who died there (n = 330); and (3) males 60 and over who were discharged from the facility (n = 287). Since older people sent to the Long Island Almshouse often ended their lives there, the first two samples represent the typical permanent aged population at the island in the first half of the twentieth century. Although no records of older discharged females were available, those for males make it possible to test whether discharged populations differed markedly from deceased ones. In addition, a series of cohort subsamples of deceased men and women will be used to examine change over time.[20]

The evidence in the samples leads to the following general arguments:

1. The twentieth century witnessed the final development of an old age nursing facility out of a nineteenth-century almshouse setting.
2. This nursing or custodial facility served a highly ethnic, completely working-class population, in contradistinction to the Yankee charities.
3. As in the private homes, the lack of an effective family network was the chief factor in precipitating institutionalization.

The Long Island inmates shared certain striking characteristics: 96 percent were white, consistent with the racial makeup of Boston itself. Nearly 60 percent were foreign-born, in contrast to the population served in the Yankee private homes, and even the native-born almshouse inmates tended to report foreign ancestry. The male population contained deviant subpopulations: alcoholics and petty criminals. Nonetheless, "rounders" were not typical: 92 percent of the deceased men and women had never been to Long Island before their sixtieth birthday.[21] Males and females did, however, differ in important respects.

Almsmen

Men averaged 66 years of age at first admission. Most (68 percent) were admitted only once; about one-fifth made three or more journeys on the *Bradlee*, generally a sign of alcoholism.[22] From last admission to death, these older men spent a mean of 3.2 years in the institution; since a number were terminally ill upon admission and died soon thereafter, the almshouse commitment was quite lengthy for many inmates. These various measures, except for the term of confinement, tended to increase across the period. For example, age of entry in the last cohort (1941–51) averaged 68 years, compared with 65 in 1908–18. The rise in age of admission followed from the expansion of outdoor relief as new forms of welfare allowed older people to find support outside the almshouse.[23]

Although the medical staff asserted that the inmates were sick and that most, when admitted, "went at once into the Hospital," only a minority of inmates resided in the hospital. In fact, the percentage of the aged receiving hospital care was decidedly less than the percentages for younger groups. In the special census of 31 January 1905, about 26 percent of the male population under 65 was receiving direct hospital care, as opposed to 12 percent of men aged 65 and over. In 1916–17, 37 percent of all males admitted were assigned on arrival to the hospital, but only 29 percent of males 65 and over.[24]

In the sample of deceased males, most (57 percent) were given simple custodial care, although nearly all spent some time in the hospital section, at least in the period just before death. The facility functioned for old people as a nursing home, with degrees of incapacity represented by assignment to different wards.

Table V-4 illustrates the predominance of the foreign-born among Long Island aged men. Across the period 1900–1950, 52 percent of the almsmen were foreign-born; as late as the 1940s, about half had been born outside the United States. The cohorts reflect the changing ethnicity of the aged poor in Boston. The intriguing fact that the percentage of foreign-born men remained quite high even in the later cohort actually corresponds with the census figures analyzed in Chapter II, which demonstrated the overwhelming importance of the foreign-born in Boston's aged population throughout the first half of the twentieth century. As seen both in the

Table V–4.
Birthplaces of Deceased Almsmen by Cohort and Demicentury

Birthplace	Cohorts				
	1908–18 (%)	1919–29 (%)	1930–40 (%)	1941–51 (%)	1900–1950 (%)
Boston	18	26	27	27	25
Other United States	28	20	23	23	23
Ireland	30	24	18	14	21
Italy	3	5	15	10	9
Other Foreign	21	26	17	27	22[a]

SOURCE: Long Island case records, 1900–1950: n = 339, 4 missing.
NOTE: Rounding errors cause deviations from 100 percent in totals for columns.
[a] Fifteen percent from Canada (primarily Maritimes), England, and Scotland.

aggregate population and among these almsmen, increases in the number of Italian and other foreign-born males in later cohorts compensated for declining percentages of Irish-born men. Table II-2 in Chapter II indicates that the Long Island Almshouse population faithfully reflected the real proportions of the foreign-born among Boston's aged; that is, it was not an institution distinguished by a disproportionate concentration of old male foreigners. (Nationally, on the other hand, the male inmate population *was* disproportionately foreign.) In Boston in 1910, the foreign-born made up 54 percent of men aged 65 and over, equal to the percentage of foreign almsmen 60 and over in the 1908–18 cohort (Table V-4). In 1930, the foreign-born constituted 53 percent, and, in 1950, 55 percent, of the city's aged male population, again practically equivalent to almshouse levels.[25]

Although the foreign-born represented a proportionate part of the inmate population, men of foreign *background* exceeded city averages. Table II-2 in Chapter II shows that less than 10 percent of the native-born aged (both men and women) reported a foreign parent in 1910, and about 21 per-

cent so responded in 1940. At the almshouse, however, foreign parentage dominated among native-born inmates. Approximately 88 percent of all men were either foreign-born
or had foreign parentage. Forty percent of the fathers and 50
percent of the mothers of native-born men had been born in
Ireland. Irish and Irish American men constituted 44 percent
of the almshouse population. Predominately and disproportionately foreign in background if not birth, the aged male
inmate population made Long Island Almshouse into an institution for the Irish. By 1900 the immigrants of the nineteenth century had reached old age, and the impoverished,
alcoholic, and isolated among them ended their days in the
poorhouse. Thirty years later, the American-born sons and
daughters of this ethnic group came here to die.[26]

The identification of the almshouse with foreigners, and
specifically with the Irish people of Boston, had great political significance. The Protestant welfare system dominant
in the city at the turn of the century, and typified by the
Yankee homes we have studied, made the poorhouse the
place—the odious place—where the Irish could be sent
when they broke down in old age. The welfare theories of
the Protestant elite demanded the restriction of public relief
and used a disreputable almshouse to force the poor to support themselves and not rely on the state. Such policies directly injured the Irish community in Boston, and that community's hatred of the almshouse emerged in the political
struggle for new public relief programs for the aged. As we
shall see, Boston's ethnic communities demanded new and
generous *outdoor* relief programs, that would reduce the burden of support for the aged in families and protect the ethnic aged from the almshouse.

Evidence from the Yankee homes demonstrated that no
occupation established an impregnable defense against having to seek relief in old age. Older men in the almshouse
certainly found less security than their Yankee coevals in
work, since, as Table V-5 shows, they were likely to hold

Table V–5.
Occupations of Deceased Almsmen, 1900–1950

Occupation	%
None	3
LBC	57
SBC	34
LWC	6
Total	100

SOURCE: Long Island case records, 1900–1950: n = 344, 9 missing.

inferior positions. Occupational proportions showed remarkably little change over time when subdivided by cohort.
In each cohort, between 50 and 60 percent of the men reported a LBC occupation and about one-third a SBC occupation (the latter figure may be exaggerated in the records).
Contrary to expectation, white-collar percentages did not
increase; the levels in successive cohorts were 12, 4, 5, and
7 percent. Comparison with Stephan Thernstrom's estimates of Boston's occupational structure between 1880 and
1930 reveals that during the same period Long Island exhibited a disproportionately high percentage of LBC workers,
a low percentage of white-collar workers, and about the
same percentage of SBC workers.[27] We know that the older
worker could often maintain employment in SBC occupations (Table III-6); in addition, a few older men may have
turned to LBC work when they lost their principal occupations (Table III-7). However, the findings in Chapter III
indicate that, by the mid-twentieth century, men had grown
old in white-collar occupations, and therefore a higher proportion of aged men worked in them. Since this cohort effect
should be operating, the absence of a sizable increase in
white-collar occupations at Long Island argues for a class
interpretation of the institution. The nineteenth-century
almshouse functioned as a relief agency for a broad spectrum

of workers; such a role fit the punitive theory of indoor relief developed in that century. By the twentieth century, Long Island had lost this more general function and been reserved for the "lower orders."[28] Since we know that white-collar workers did not escape poverty and dependency, we must presume that they received help elsewhere—for example, in the Yankee private homes. There were a few similar homes for other ethnic groups, and, as shall be seen, alternative sources of support developed as public outdoor relief for the aged expanded in Boston during the 1920s, relief available to immigrant ethnic groups. The latter expansion probably offers the best explanation for the deficiency of former white-collar employees at Long Island.

Several additional features of the occupational records deserve note. Irish and Italian men dominated LBC occupations. Canadians and other foreigners predominated among skilled workers, and New England–born men ruled the small LWC catagory. SBC workers tended to enter the institution at a later age than their LBC counterparts.

But it was family structure, regardless of occupational category, that dictated institutionalization. For skilled and unskilled, Yankee and Irish, the worst flaw was to have no family.[29] Twenty-nine percent of the Long Island men reported single status, 31 percent married, and 36 percent widowed. Although these percentages show dramatic changes over time (a decline in married or widowed and an increase in single men), in no instance did a distribution approximate the normal patterns for Boston's old men, as shown in Table II-3. In the Boston population, most men 65 and over were married, whereas only about one-third of those at Long Island had claim to the company and assistance of a wife. The extraordinarily high percentages of widowed and single men at Long Island point to isolation from family as the determinant factor in institutionalization. Widowed and married men reported a mean of 1.9 children; when single men are included, the average number falls to 1.3. Thirty-nine percent of the aged inmates reported that they had no children. These data cannot be regarded as perfectly accurate, but they may actually exaggerate the number of children capable of support.[30] The small number of children stands out all the more when one considers the high birth rates in the ethnic populations from which these men were drawn. Few additional relatives were recorded. These older men reported an average of only 1.3 relatives living in Massachusetts and therefore accessible for assistance.[31] Twenty percent would, like Michael Baldwin, die unnoticed, for they had "no relatives or friends."[32]

The Almswomen

Their ethnic sisters fared no better. Study of the female population at Long Island reinforces the ethnic, occupational, and familial results for men.[33] All age measures for the deceased female population exceeded those for men. Women averaged 70 years at first admission, and 75 at death. As with men, these measures rose across time. Conversely, time spent in the institution (from last admission to death) declined rapidly, from 3.2 to 1.8 years, reflecting the increased ability of older women to use public outdoor relief and postpone commitment to the almshouse.

Most women (84 percent) were admittted only once, and only 6 percent three or more times, indicating no large alcoholic class among them. Again medical treatment was temporary. Women who survived the initial hospital admission found themselves assigned to custodial care until a final crisis lead to readmission to the hospital. Even those who remained hospitalized usually resided in wards where treatment amounted to nursing home care. The medical staff described these facilities as an "outpatient department of infirm old men and women, inmates of the almshouse section who must be provided with extra care and attention."[34]

Although the ethnicity of almswomen largely reflected

Table V–6.
Birthplaces of Deceased Almswomen by Cohort and
Demicentury

	Cohorts				
Birthplace	1908–18 (%)	1919–29 (%)	1930–40 (%)	1941–51 (%)	1900–1950 (%)
Boston	8	22	20	25	16
Other United States	11	15	15	22	13
Ireland	57	32	28	19	42
Italy	2	3	9	3	3
Canada	12	16	15	13	14
Other Foreign	10	12	15	19	12

SOURCE: Long Island case records, 1900–1950: n = 320, 10 missing.
NOTE: Rounding errors cause deviations from 100 percent in totals for columns.

the ethnic composition of Boston's aged population, as did that of their male peers, important differences existed between males and females at the Island. Long Island women reported foreign nativity more often than almsmen and more often than their aged female counterparts in Boston's population. In 1910 foreign-born women made up 53 percent of Boston's female population 65 and over; in 1930, 51 percent; and in 1950, 51 percent.[35] As illustrated in Table V-6, 71 percent of the almswomen (60 and over) had been born in foreign countries, and only in the last cohort did the foreign-born among the inmates approximate the foreign-born proportion in Boston itself.

Indeed, while the male inmate population differed from the national pattern in having a relatively small proportion of the foreign-born, the female population exceeded the national level.[36] In addition, male inmates roughly reflected the proportions of foreign-born and native-born among aged men in Boston, whereas female inmates came from a very particular, foreign part of the aged female population of the city.

Even as the native-born element increased in the Long Island female population, it disguised foreign ancestry. Of the minority of native-born women, 68 percent reported at least one foreign-born parent and 58 percent an Irish parent. Women of foreign birth or ancestry made up 93 percent of all women who died at Long Island in the half century from 1900 to 1950, and Irish or Irish American women were an extraordinary 59 percent of that population.

The obvious prominence of old Irish woman in the almshouse demands explanation. Long Island functioned straightforwardly as an institution for foreign-born aged women, and in the early twentieth century, aged Irish-born women virtually defined its population. The Irish-born population in Massachusetts had, as we have seen in Chapter II, begun to age dramatically at the end of the nineteenth century. The decline in the percentage of Irish-born almswomen across the twentieth century corresponds with the diminishing importance of the Irish in the aged population as a whole. But two anomalies remain: first, in all cohorts the percentage of Irish almswomen appears markedly greater than the percentage of Irish in the aged female population in general; second, other foreign groups only partially compensated for the declining significance of the Irish in later cohorts.

What explains these aberrations? In Irish and Canadian immigration to Boston, women predominated; this predominance did not hold among Italian immigrants. In the early twentieth century, before the New Deal, when old Irish women constituted the largest group of aged likely to need assistance, private charities controlled relief for the dependent aged. These charities, prone to nativism and anti-Catholicism, generally rejected Irish-born females in need. (After the New Deal, ethnicity did not disqualify, and more Irish women could get assistance outside the almshouse.) But the most useful explanation may lie in marital status. Since the number of Irish women in Boston exceeded that of Irish men, the female's position in the marriage market was weak. As analysis of the almswomen's family structure will demonstrate, high percentages of spinsters and widows among the Irish distinguished them from other ethnic groups. Unlikely to have many other relatives in the United States, at a disadvantage in the marriage market whether widowed or single, and seen as unworthy by the powerful private charities, Irish-born women in Boston may have been particularly vulnerable to institutionalization in old age.[37]

Frederick Bushee captured this phenomenon in 1903 in his *Ethnic Factors in the Population of Boston*: "among the Irish there was a large proportion of single immigrant women who come to this country when young and for years probably gain fair employment but small earnings. As time passes, employment becomes more difficult to obtain, and having no one to care for them, these women find their refuge in the almshouse."[38]

None of the almshouse ethnic groups escaped vulnerability by reason of occupation. Members of the distinctly foreign Long Island female population were even more likely than their Yankee sisters to have been LBC workers, especially domestics. In fact, while later cohorts of Yankee women enjoyed access to some LWC occupations (see Chapter IV), the Long Island women never escaped the trap of domestic toil. Table V-7 details the unpleasant occupational history of these Irish girls grown old. Four important themes emerge.

First, almshouse women worked. Even with generous corrections for the reporting of past rather than present occupations, the labor force participation of the inmates greatly exceeded normal levels for their age group (never higher than 5 percent in the first half of the twentieth century). The irony that extraordinarily industrious people ended up in the almshouse, supposedly reserved for the shiftless, was surely lost on these inmates.

Second, the Island frankly served the working class of Boston. Almshouse women worked in LBC occupations much

Table V–7.

Occupations of Deceased Almswomen by Cohort and
Demicentury

	Cohorts				
Occupation	1908–18 (%)	1919–29 (%)	1930–40 (%)	1941–51 (%)	1900–1950 (%)
None	12	12	17	23	14
LBC	75	83	68	69	76
SBC	12	3	15	8	10
LWC	0	2	0	0	0

SOURCE: Long Island case records, 1900–1950: n = 312, 18 missing.

NOTE: Rounding errors cause deviations from 100 percent in totals for columns.

more commonly than their coevals in the Boston population. The small increases in white-collar employment among older women during the twentieth century do not appear at all in the Long Island records. In Chapter III it was found that women 65 and over worked as bookkeepers, saleswomen, and teachers by 1940 and 1950. One-third of the Yankee women in the 1940s cohort of the HAW reported white-collar occupations (Chapter IV). But no such cohort effect appeared among almshouse women. The city awarded Long Island to its ethnic domestic servants, waitresses, and seamstresses in their old age. The case records make it clear that it did so only when such women became incapable of further work.

Third, the white-collar woman must have had other resources when she became destitute or sick in old age. Institutions like the HAW accepted her if she had a Yankee background or met some other standard of respectability. A Catholic home might have room for a good Catholic woman. Social workers, repeatedly emphasizing the class nature of the almshouse, described the repugnance for it among the "respectable." But unworthiness seems to have been defined by a brogue and a history of laboring with a mop. Charity workers undoubtedly sought private and public support for respectable women (even the city's relief officers had funds at their disposal for the "better" pauper). These sources may have kept some white-collar women from ending up at Long Island.

Finally, the principal change in the distribution over time was the increase in the category "none," which included all housewives. The percentages of inmates reporting no occupation rose from 12 percent in the 1908–18 cohort to 23 percent in the 1940s group. This trend followed exactly the pattern noted in Chapter III and analyzed for HAW clients in Chapter IV. No change occurred before the 1930s cohort. Increases appeared when public welfare policies provided more older women, especially widows, with enough income that they were not obliged to enter the labor market after the loss of a male provider.

These plain statistics reverberate with the history of old age in the twentieth century: the widowed housewife appears as the problem at the center of the crisis over old age dependency. Among the Long Island women as among the clients of the HAW, marital status significantly affected occupational status; single women, although about a quarter of all women, were one-half of the higher SBC category.[39] The difficulties women trained as housewives encountered in seeking work was recognized in the late nineteenth century; Mary Roberts Smith noted that such domestic occupations "unfit women for self support."[40] But the almshouse experience also indicates that marriage was a gamble women were wise to take. For what really distinguished those who were vulnerable in old age from those who were not was the size and strength of the family network.

The summary of Long Island women's marital status and family structure in Table V-8 shows that widows predominated among female inmates; this predominance follows precisely the pattern observed previously in Boston's entire

Table V–8.
Marital Status and Family Structure among Deceased Almswomen by Cohort and Demicentury

	Cohorts				
Marital status/Family structure	*1908–18*	*1919–29*	*1930–40*	*1941–51*	*1900–1950*
% Single	21	22	27	19	23
% Married	13	10	17	31	17
% Widowed	66	65	55	50	59
Mean Number of Children	1.2	0.8	1.3	1.9	1.2
(including Single Women)	(0.8)	(0.6)	(0.9)	(1.5)	(0.8)
Mean No. of Massachusetts Relatives	0.7	0.8	1.1	1.4	0.9

SOURCE: Long Island case records, 1900–1950: n = 314, 16 missing.

150

aged female population. However, the percentage of single women exceeds that found in Boston (already extraordinarily high) in every cohort but the last. The Irish and New England backgrounds of the women make the spinsterhood levels plausible, since women outnumbered men in these ethnic groups. The statistical measures vary significantly by nativity.[41] Native-born women displayed an even higher rate of spinsterhood than the foreign-born: 32 percent were single, a level consistent with that found among Yankee women at the HAW. Irish (22 percent) and Canadian (27 percent) spinsterhood suggests the results of sexual imbalance in immigrant populations. This imbalance was most powerful in its effects in the early cohorts, when Irish women constituted almost the whole of the Long Island female population.

Of women who had been married, more than half reported that they had no living children, a remarkable figure. Since almswomen composed only a very small segment of the population of older women, their childlessness is plausible, but even if they concealed a relative from the authorities, their isolation from any family network able and willing to help them appears manifestly in the records. On average, the old women recorded less than one relative in the state; 39 percent said that they had no relatives in Massachusetts, a figure very similar to that provided by the women of the HAW. These data point to family lives even more bereft than those of the Long Island men, providing some confirmation of the adage that women were more likely than men to be accepted by a relative, for a woman had to be singularly unattached to be deported to the Island. In the case of 79-year-old Emiline Brady, the city social worker informed almshouse officials that "If discharged, there is no one to care for her." The social worker hoped "that she may be kept at Long Island." Ella Cassidy was, by order of the private Associated Charities, not to be discharged, for there was "No one to support her."[42]

The data also confirm the findings of Michael Katz in his

study of the nineteenth-century poorhouse. Katz concludes that "the absence of a spouse or children . . . deprived working class people of the key support they required in times of unemployment, sickness, or old age." This was the fundmental flaw of a dependent older person, the almshouse man or woman, or even the aging Yankee clerk: "the worst [circumstance] was to be without a spouse or children in old age."[43]

Conclusions

The transformation of the almshouse into an old age home had important implications in the campaign for social security. Nothing in the records of the Long Island Almshouse indicates that the rate of institutionalization increased between 1880 and 1930; in fact, the proportion of older Bostonians confined to the almshouse remained the same. But as any visitor could plainly see, Long Island now held *only* old people and dissipated alcoholics. Once the central institution in a punitive welfare system that refused outdoor relief to the unemployed, the almshouse now served to board the decrepit aged and to dry out alcoholics. Once a place where the unemployed, sick, retarded, orphaned, and pregnant could be sent, the poorhouse now provided rude stages of custodial care for old people.

These old people were almost invariably without families. In the ethnic communities of Boston, an older person who fell sick and had no relatives to rely on was vulnerable to institutionalization in the almshouse. Even though it had changed from a general relief institution into an old age home, Long Island remained a repulsive alternative. Realizing its founders' intention that the house be so unpleasant as to force the lazy to work, the poorhouse offered the aged a crowded, filthy, and vice-ridden environment with facilities for the dismemberment of dead paupers in full view of the living inmates' sitting porches. Almshouse care cost city officials more per recipient than other forms of welfare, and these recipients, with few relatives in the voting population of Boston, exercised little influence over the city treasury. Little wonder that Long Island never became a "comfortable and peaceful home for old people."[44]

Other older people did have family ties in the ethnic communities of the city. These older people did not escape dependency; those among them who lived too long or got sick, fired, or widowed had to turn to their families for help. Facing a welfare system dominated by a Protestant elite that resisted outdoor relief and sent dependent older people to the almshouse, Irish and other ethnic families could avoid the institutionalization of their dependent aged only by supporting them with family resources. Many families had few resources to spare, and in any case the burdens of even minimal nursing care might be beyond the resources of adult children. We should not be surprised if these relatives spoke to their political representatives and demanded from the city true relief, without the insult of the poorhouse.

Chapter VI
Children of the State: The Aged on Outdoor Relief

An alternative to the almshouse did exist in Boston, in the form of outdoor or noninstitutional relief. In 1920 noninstitutional public relief aided perhaps twice as many aged men and women as resided in the Long Island Almshouse. Across the next decade a striking expansion took place in both the number of older people on the rolls and their average benefits. Well before the New Deal, Boston's public system began to provide more older people with assistance without demanding that they enter the poorhouse.

Conventional histories of old age argue that the New Deal's Social Security Act inaugurated relief for the aged. Such a view confuses full maturity with origin. Following the expansion of city welfare in the 1920s, the Massachusetts Old Age Assistance Act (1930) spurred still greater increases in the number and proportion of the aged on public relief in Boston. Federal legislation, beginning with the Social Security Act in 1935, accelerated the trend toward larger welfare rolls and financed still more generous average benefits. By 1950 trends quite visible in the Boston of the 1920s had resulted in a dramatic social change: the majority of the aged—once workers or supported within the family—were now public pensioners. Momentous as the New Deal policies were (for example, in undercutting the labor force participation of older men), they evolved from a focus on the aged already apparent in the urban welfare of the 1920s.

In this chapter we will examine the extension of public relief for the aged in Boston, coming to grips with the nature, extent, and level of city aid before and after the New Deal. But the primary question is *why* public welfare for the elderly expanded in the early twentieth-century city. I believe that the answer lies in class and ethnic politics, an interpretation that runs counter to the traditional reading of the origins of welfare programs in the United States.[1]

For most historians, sociologists, and political scientists, the United States stands out as an exception to the general rule that working-class pressure has been instrumental in the creation of the welfare state. Noting the opposition of trade union leaders in the American Federation of Labor to many state welfare schemes, and the absence of an American political party dominated by labor, these scholars look elsewhere for an explanation of the rise of the welfare state. Generally, middle-class reform societies are given credit for bringing welfare needs to the attention of the American public, and politicians, sensitive to the effects of the depression, implemented the programs. In recent research the "state" and its officials assume a more independent and influential role in shaping welfare legislation.

In the Boston of the 1920s, this was not how it worked. Irish working-class constituencies dominated city politics, and their mayors, councilmen, and public welfare officers set relief policy. As the records of the Long Island Almshouse suggest, such constituencies had good reason to ask that outdoor relief be used to assist the aged in their families because the unpleasant alternative was to send them to the poorhouse.

It is unlikely that Boston was unique in this working-class politics. It can be shown that in numerous states organized labor strongly supported the movement for state old age pensions. It made sense for labor to petition for noncontributory public pensions, and in the 1920s trade union officials and political representatives from working-class districts emphatically demanded them. What set Boston apart was the great success of this movement in the implementation of generous relief standards, an achievement amply demonstrated in the municipal welfare records.

Municipal Welfare, 1920–1950

Before the 1930s Boston municipal officials exercised nearly complete and very jealous control over the city's welfare monies. Under the Massachusetts welfare laws, towns and cities conducted and paid for public charity with minimal direction from the state. Only in the mothers' aid program, an early form of aid to dependent children established in 1913, did the state provide considerable funds and guidelines. Boston's welfare officials, the Overseers of the Public Welfare (previously the Overseers of the Poor), selected by the mayor for terms of three years, presided over a relief budget larger than that of any American city except New York and Detroit, reaching $2.5 million in 1929.[2]

Within their province the Overseers chose to provide aid primarily to old people and children. Such beneficiaries made up the bulk of all recipients and consumed most of the city's relief funds. Increases in both the size and the cost of the elderly relief caseload marked the 1920s. But the increases do not prove that the rate of poverty among the aged had increased; instead, as will be seen, the city appears to have been more willing to provide relief to citizens once considered ineligible and, therefore, previously dependent on work or family for support.

Through much of the first half of the century, the elderly made up the largest and second most expensive group in the caseload of the Overseers. Indeed, rather like welfare today, pre–New Deal outdoor relief functioned primarily to provide for old people (principally women) and to aid female-headed families. In 1906 the Overseers reported: "For many years past by far the larger part of our beneficiaries have been widows with young children, or old men and women too feeble to work." In 1923 the Boston Finance Commission (BFC) stated: "It has been estimated that 85 per cent of the poor cases [who were not women with children] are aged women, living in single rooms." The next year the BFC's special study of families aided by the Overseers led to similar conclusions about the proportions and sex of the aged in the caseload: "A large proportion of those receiving regular aid from the overseers are elderly, and most of these are women. Many of them are widows whose relatives are dead or unable to care for them; others have been wage earners, but are now incapacitated or unable to earn more than a pittance." In an interesting analysis of 100 of these elderly clients, the BFC painted a small still life of the old age welfare system before the New Deal: only 25 percent had received relief before they were aged; only 6 percent were presently married; and half lived alone.[3]

In 1918 the Overseers first published a description of the "causes of dependency." These data, published between 1918 and 1931, reveal the central place of the old in the welfare caseload. Table VI-1 displays the causes listed in the 1918 analysis of 3,072 "selected" cases. These cases made up about 75 percent of the total number of persons aided during the year and included mothers' aid, for which the state shared costs.[4]

Initially the Overseers confounded old age and sickness and failed to separate mothers' aid cases from the remainder of the caseload. Although the officers never defined "old age," after 1920 they distinguished it from sickness and provided separate information for mothers' aid. Table VI-2 summarizes these data in an invaluable outline of an urban welfare system before the New Deal.

Even if we exclude persons 65 and over who were classified

Children of the State

Table VI–1.
"Causes of Dependency" among Selected Boston Outdoor Relief
Cases, 1918

Cause	%
Sickness or Old Age	39
Death of Wage-Earner[a]	37
Desertion or Nonsupport	11
Tuberculosis	5
Other Diseases	5
Unemployment of Wage-Earner	2
Disability	1
Intemperance	1
	(n = 3,072)

SOURCE: "Annual Report of the Overseers of the Poor Department" (AROPD),
Documents of the City of Boston (DCB), 1918, vol. 2, no. 21, p. 3.
NOTE: Rounding errors cause deviation from 100 percent in column total.
[a] Largely mothers' aid cases.

as sick, unemployed, deserted, or widowed, the aged constituted approximately 35 percent of the dependent aid caseload during the 1920s, and about 28 percent of the entire
caseload. Since the elderly made up some proportion of the
other categories and also dominated a relief group for
whom the Overseers dispensed special trust funds, the aged
can be fairly estimated as making up about one-third of the
city's poor relief recipients throughout the decade.[5]

Although the proportion of the elderly among recipients
remained constant, the actual number of aged being assisted
increased rapidly, rising from approximately 1,200 cases in
the early 1920s to nearly 2,000 by 1928 and more than 3,000
in 1931. This increase in the number of beneficiaries cannot be explained by increases in the number of older persons
in the city. If we take 1921 and 1930 as limits and assume
that the aged were one-third of all recipients, the number
of old people aided rose from 1,164 to 2,441, an increase of
about 100 percent. By way of comparison, between 1920 and

Table VI–2.
Major "Causes of Dependency" among Boston Outdoor Relief Cases, 1921–1931

Year	Cause of Dependency among Dependent Aid Cases				Dependent Aid Cases (n)	Dependent and Mothers' Aid Cases[a] (n)	Aged as % of Caseload
	Old Age (%)	Sickness (%)	Unemployment (%)	Desertion/ Death of Wage-Earner (%)			
1921	51	14	17	17	1,978	3,492	29
1922	32	11	41	14	3,025	4,416	NA[b]
1923	34	15	34	15	3,711	5,145	26
1924	40	14	20	21	3,384	4,680	29
1925	39	14	25	18	3,608	4,807	29
1926	39	14	24	17	3,918	5,085	30
1927	35	16	22	23	4,118	5,228	28
1928	35	15	25	19	4,766	5,813	29
1929	35	14	29	16	5,473	6,464	30
1930	33	18	26	22	6,347	7,322	29
1931	28	13	41	16	10,135	11,182	25

SOURCES: "AROPD", *DCB*, 1919, vol. 2, no. 21, p. 3; "Fifty-Sixth AROPD," *DCB*, 1920, vol. 2, no. 21, p. 3; "Fifty-Seventh AROPD," *DCB*, 1921, vol. 2, no. 18, p. 3; "Fifty-Eighth Annual Report of the Overseers of the Public Welfare" "AROPW," *DCB*, 1922, vol. 2, no. 18, p. 3; "Fifty-Ninth AROPW," *DCB*, 1923, vol. 2, no. 18, p. 4; "Sixtieth AROPW," *DCB*, 1924, vol. 2, no. 18, p. 4; "Sixty-First AROPW," *DCB*, 1925, vol. 2, no. 19, p. 4; "Sixty-Second AROPW," *DCB*, 1926, vol. 2, no. 19, p. 4; "Sixty-Third AROPW," *DCB*, 1927, vol. 2, no. 23, p. 4; "Sixty-Fourth AROPW," *DCB*, 1928, vol. 2, no. 23, p. 4; "Sixty-Fifth AROPW," *DCB*, 1929, vol. 2, no. 23, p. 4; "Sixty-Sixth AROPW," *DCB*, 1930, vol. 2, no. 23, p. 4; "Sixty-Seventh AROPW," *DCB*, 1931, vol. 2, no. 23, p. 4.

ª Dependent aid and mothers' aid combined; this total excluded only cases given grants from special funds. Special funds aided about 300 cases each year, and the recipients were primarily aged women.

ᵇ Cannot be calculated since not all dependent cases were analyzed.

1930 the number of persons 65 and over in Boston rose from 33,100 to 42,637, a change of only about 30 percent.[6]

The rising number of aged persons receiving public assistance appears to indicate that the rate of poverty among Boston's elderly had risen sharply during the 1920s. But such a conclusion is premature. Two factors determine public dependency among the aged: labor force participation and family status. Our previous analyses of these factors in the Boston population indicated that labor force participation among older males declined only slightly during the early twentieth century, and rose among older women. Demographic data showed that the percentage of married persons among older men and women in Boston, the group least likely to require public assistance, *increased* between 1920 and 1930. Hence, other things being equal, the overall rate of poverty among Boston's elderly should not have risen rapidly. Finally, dramatic increases in the traditional forms of overt public dependency should have led to increases in the number of almshouse commitments, yet these did not occur.

A more persuasive argument considers the possibility that the Overseers redefined "deserving need." Since the individual case records of their outdoor relief are not available, we can only infer that Boston's public welfare officials became more receptive to the aged who had adult children or other relatives, or who were capable of some work. In fact, some evidence strongly suggests that the Overseers did not face a greater proportion of aged who met the old standards of need, but rather decided that a greater proportion deserved relief. The evidence lies in the fact that Boston was more generous in *all* categories of public assistance. Table VI-2 shows that the *nonaged* caseload doubled during the 1920s, although the city's population did not increase; the entire caseload, aged and nonaged alike, rose in this period, a clear sign that the Overseers tended to be more liberal in their grants.[7]

That such generosity, rather than poverty among the aged,

explains the increasing percentage of aged on the rolls is confirmed by data indicating that the average amount of relief given older beneficiaries rose during the 1920s. By a rough estimate, aid given at the end of the decade was about twice that received by the average case in 1921. Although never munificent, aid in the late 1920s edged closer to the "adequacy" standard that some social workers argued for. In 1923 the BFC stated that the average weekly grant had once been $2.00 (in kind) in the summer and $3.00 in winter, without regard for the size of the assisted family. This stipend, so low that subsistence was hardly possible, presumed additional support from other sources. The BFC argued that the Commonwealth of Massachusetts had imposed standards of adequacy and adjustment for family size in the mothers' aid law and that these standards had spilled over into other forms of public aid, increasing city expenditure. The commission reported that the Overseers now intended to provide aid "'adequate' to support the family." Nonetheless, dependent aid in the early 1920s rarely exceeded an average rate of about $2.50 per week per person, or about $130 per year for an aged beneficiary. In 1924 the BFC conducted a special study of a group of dependent aid cases, concluded that a large proportion of these were elderly, and stated that the "usual aid granted them is $3.00 a week," or $156 per year. The commission added that "some of the old people are living with friends and have a fair amount of comfort"; others got additional support from private charities. Among 100 aged beneficiaries, only 8 relied solely on Overseers' aid, 10 worked irregularly, and 24 were assisted by friends, 25 by charitable agencies, and the remainder presumably by relatives. Over the next five years, the average grant rose substantially. In 1926 Maurice Taylor of the Federated Jewish Charities stated that "the Overseers have increased their grants to the aged, and, in most instances, the Overseers believe the income of those aided by them is adequate." In 1929 the social worker at the HAM stated that an average grant from the Overseers to an elderly man was $5 per week.[8]

Aggregate data on expenditures by the Overseers verify the trend toward higher relief across the decade. From 1923 to 1928 the number of cases carried under dependent aid (of whom about one-third were elderly) increased by 13 percent, while the amount of relief granted increased by 46 percent. The average yearly grant for all cases other than mothers' aid rose as follows: in 1917, it was $83; in 1921, $124; in 1925, $215; and in 1929, $271.[9]

During the 1920s, then, two trends in the city's relief system benefited the aged. The proportion of the elderly population aided rose, and the level of relief given clearly increased. Rather than being consequences of increasing poverty among old people, these trends apparently resulted from new definitions of need and the level of support an old person deserved to receive. The increasingly liberal attitude of the Boston Overseers—a result of Irish political power hardly observed with approbation by Brahmin welfare officials at the state level—prefigured the triumph of the welfare state for the aged in the New Deal. Indeed, the onset of the New Deal would not create such a state but would merely bring it to maturity, first broadening the system and then deepening its generosity.

Boston and
the New Deal

A new deal for old people began in Massachusetts well before the election of Franklin Delano Roosevelt. The relatively quiet expansion of the municipal welfare system during the 1920s had been accompanied by a widely publicized campaign for state old age pensions. This movement, whose origins, constituency, and purposes are reviewed in the conclusion of this chapter, sought special state-funded welfare programs for the elderly. In 1930 the campaign achieved a partial victory in the passage of an old age assistance act (OAA), which committed the state to assist towns and cities in aiding the elderly. The legislation, modeled on the mothers' aid program, stipulated that "adequate assistance" must be given to needy citizens 70 and over who had resided in Massachusetts for 20 years immediately before their seventieth birthday. Although the assistance had to be "sufficient to provide suitable and dignified care," preferably in the old person's own home, local overseers remained in charge of determining the level of aid and were admonished in the act to test the ability of relatives to support the applicant. Except for the promise of one-third reimbursement by the state and language that could be read as sanctioning strong state supervision, no essential differences existed between OAA and traditional municipal poor relief.[10]

Although mothers' aid, with similar provisions, had increased benefit levels, the OAA legislation did not immediately have this effect. The Commonwealth's Department of Public Welfare (DPW), which had been granted supervisory powers of potential significance, chose not to exercise them. In fact, the DPW and its commissioner, an adherent of the welfare principles of Boston's Protestant elite, vigorously opposed the political movement that forced old age pensions upon the department. Commissioner Richard Conant, appointed by Governor Calvin Coolidge in 1921, had on several occasions expressed his hostility toward state aid for the elderly; his advisory board, the leaders of Boston's major private welfare agencies, and social workers from those agencies joined him in this opposition. Brahmin social welfare leaders, fearful of the powerful Boston public system, which was dominated by ethnic politicians, resisted the encroachment of public welfare onto the domain of "social service", i.e., investigation and counselling of the poor by social workers. Rightly suspicious of the inherently political nature of public welfare programs, contemptuous of the public system's ethnic, working-class, and Catholic beneficiaries (whom they regarded as deserving of their fate), and insistent that social service offered more to the poor than a mere handout, these welfare leaders attacked extensions of state welfare; when confronted by *faits accomplis*, they made little attempt to enforce adequacy provisions on local officials.[11]

Not until 1936, when state legislation brought Massachusetts in line with the federal Social Security Act, did the state demand a minimum grant ($30 per month) from the local overseers; only through state mandates in the statutes of 1941 and 1943 were budgetary standards imposed on the local poor relief officers.[12] Table VI-3 displays data on the number of elderly people aided and the level of benefits provided in Boston; the data clearly indicate the continuous expansion in the numbers aided and the interruption of the 1920s trend toward more generous benefits. In Boston's 1931 public welfare report (covering the last year before the introduction of state old age assistance), we can estimate the number of "old" clients in the city's dependent aid system at about 3,500. In 1936, before the imposition of federal standards under the Social Security Act, and when 70 remained the minimum age for OAA, over 5,000 elderly Bostonians received OAA, and another 2,900 received dependent aid. The first effect of OAA was to accelerate the already rapid expansion of public old age benefits for the aged. However, the state program did not encourage continued increases in the average benefit. In 1931 the average annual dependent aid benefit was about $290.00. If we correct the deflation, the 1936 OAA benefit of $271.91, equaled about $299.00 in 1931 currency.[13]

Thus, the introduction of OAA reinforced the trend toward increased numbers on the rolls but did not prompt local overseers to continue to increase benefit levels. The explanation lies in a logical alternative available to city OAA bureaus, which had great difficulty during the depression in raising cash from municipal taxes. The boards used state

Table VI-3.
Assistance to Old People in Boston, 1931–1951

	Dependent Aid		Old Age Assistance			
Year	No. of "Old" Aided[a]	Average $/yr.	No. 65 and Over Aided	Average $/yr.	Average $/mo.	Average $/mo. in 1931 dollars
1931	3,489	288.59	none	—	NA	—
1936	2,870	205.00	5,159[b]	271.91	NA	NA
1939	NA	162.60	14,680	291.22	28.01[c]	31
1942	NA	166.77	17,954	323.09	29.07[c]	27
1946	1,541	231.40	15,949	487.66	42.76[c]	34
1949	>750	235.76	19,884	609.07	58.20	37
1951	NA	321.52	22,750	677.87	68.32	40

SOURCES: "Sixty-Seventh AROPW" DCB, 1931, vol. 2, no. 23, p. 4; "Seventy-Second AROPW," DCB, 1936, vol. 1, no. 23, pp. 26–27; "Seventy-Fifth AROPW," DCB, 1939, vol. 2, no. 23, pp. 2–3; "Seventy-Eighth AROPW," DCB, 1942, vol. 1, no. 23, p. 3; "Eighty-Second AROPW," DCB, 1946, vol. 1, no. 23, pp. 7, 11, 27; "Eighty-Fifth AROPW," DCB, 1949, vol. 1, no. 23, pp. 5–6, 8–14; "Eighty-Seventh AROPW," DCB, 1951, vol. 1, no. 23, pp. 7–9, 16–17; U.S. Department of Commerce, Bureau of the Census, *Historical Statistics of the United States: Colonial Times to 1970,* Pt. 1 (Washington, D.C., 1975), pp. 210–11.

  [a] Approximate figures. Figures for 1946 and 1949 are for people 65 and over.
  [b] Recipients were 70 and over.
  [c] Alton A. Linford, *Old Age Assistance in Massachusetts* (Chicago, 1949), p. 297. These average figures are for all Massachusetts; Boston levels were higher.

Table VI–4.

Percentage of Boston Welfare Spending by Program

Program	1945 (%)	1951 (%)
OAA	62	55
ADC[a]	18	21
Dependent Aid	11	16
Administrative and Other Expenses	9	8

SOURCES: "Eighty-First AROPW", *DCB, 1945,* vol. 1, no. 23, p. 3; "Eighty-Seventh AROPW," *DCB, 1951,* vol. 1, no. 23, p. 39.

NOTE: Although Boston paid about one-third of its total relief bill, it paid only about one-sixth of its OAA cost. See sources listed above and Linford, *Old Age Assistance,* pp. 169, 258.

[a] Aid to Dependent Children (formerly mothers' aid).

OAA monies to increase the rolls while keeping the benefit level at the maximum for full state reimbursement. In this manner cities received the greatest number of state tax dollars at the lowest average expense to city coffers.

Federal financial participation and state and federal laws soon forced local boards to increase benefit levels, renewing the trend toward more generous benefits that had been arrested in the early depression years. In 1939 and 1942 state requirements for benefit levels were imposed, and as Table VI-3 indicates, subsequent years show the effects of imposed standards and/or renewed prosperity and healthier city budgets. Using the monthly figures for OAA—figures that record more accurately than yearly amounts what an older person might receive—steady increases can be observed, reaching $40 per month (in 1931 dollars) for a recipient in 1951. Between 1936 and 1951 the cost of living increased by 87 percent; during the same period, the average annual OAA benefit increased by 149 percent. By the mid-1940s, Boston, which carried one-fifth of the state's OAA cases, was spending most of its welfare budget on the aged (see Table VI-4).

The city, state, and federal governments continually liberalized regulations regarding eligibility, the responsibilities of adult children for support, and the right of the OAA recipient to retain property.[14]

One reason that OAA came to cost the city so much was that the average benefit, partly funded by the federal government, became more generous. But the more important cause was the truly phenomenal increase in the number of older persons aided. The expansion rested on two programs, OAA and dependent aid. Dependent aid, often ignored as a source of relief for the elderly, included many older people, in part because aliens, not eligible for OAA, made up a significant part of the urban aged population. Although the Overseers did not always define the category "old," they reported that 16 percent of the dependent caseload met that criterion in 1935, 7 percent in 1936, and 3 percent in 1937. The decline reflects the shift to OAA among the aged population, especially after 1936, when 65 became the qualifying age. The low percentages are deceptive because the aged provided the permanent clientele of this relief program, which was characterized by "tremendous" turnover. In 1945 the Overseers reported "1,050 alien heads [of families] sixty-five years of age or over" on dependent aid and stated that for "41 percent" of the permanent part of the caseload, dependency was "due to old age." In analyzing the caseload of 31 December 1945 (n = 2,776), they found that 39 percent were 65 and over and almost 65 percent 60 and over. In a similar analysis for 1948, older people constituted 21 percent of the caseload.[15]

Although dependent aid continued to be an important source of relief for the aged, OAA created the real explosion in the rolls. While still a state program confined to those 70 and over, it underwrote an expansion of the rolls from about 3,500 old persons in 1931 to 8,000 in 1936 (Table VI-3), or an increase of 130 percent. After the passage of the Social Security Act of 1935, the age limit fell to 65, and Washington reimbursed the states for one-third of a maximum OAA grant (between federal and state grants, Boston paid only one-sixth of OAA benefits).[16] Thousands of old Bostonians joined the OAA ranks, which reached 18,000 persons in 1942, a year of relatively high employment. This figure represented a 125 percent increase from 1936.

Clearly such increases in the welfare rolls outstripped increases in the number of older people in Boston. Indeed, although the 1930 state OAA legislation and subsequent federal and state programs only accelerated a social change whose origins are quite evident in the 1920s, they transformed the experience of old age in the city. Whereas in 1920 perhaps 4 percent of Boston's aged population received outdoor relief from the Overseers (in 1930 the figure was 6 percent), by 1950, 27 percent of those 65 and over received OAA and dependent aid. This percentage does not include those receiving Social Security insurance benefits. Given national ratios of OAA to insurance recipients in 1950, we can estimate that about 25 percent of Boston's elderly population collected Social Security insurance. Thus, one-half of the urban elderly—and through them their once-pressed families—relied on state welfare. The phenomenal increase in government aid, achieved in 25 years, went straight to the center of experience for much of Boston: going "on the Old Age" became part of family life.[17]

Conclusion:
The Origins of
the Welfare State

The conventional wisdom is that the American working class, unlike its European counterpart, did not play a leading part in the creation of the welfare state. Historians of social welfare for the elderly, being particularly bedeviled by this notion, explain the agitation for public relief in the 1920s as the result of the efforts of benevolent middle-class reformers, efforts opposed by organized labor. The idea that middle-class "progressives" sustained the old age pension movement relies on still another conventional belief—that these reformers accurately perceived the inevitable degradation of the aged in industrial society. Seeing a direct relationship between increasing poverty and industrial development (or ageism), the middle class invented the welfare state solution to the new poverty rates. A sophisticated reformulation of the thesis connects the origins and shape of American welfare to the machinations of the state and its functionaries, again with little input from labor. Even Marxist accounts deny the working class its victory: the Social Security Act was designed by capitalist elites to manipulate the labor market.[18]

These views correspond poorly with the demographic, occupational, and welfare history of Boston. Any examination of the movement for old age pensions in the 1920s will show that most of the city's middle-class social service leaders who were in a position to effect reforms opposed old age pensions as an "unthinking dole." The few middle-class reformers who supported state relief were relatively insignificant actors in a campaign that depended on organized labor and working-class politicians.[19]

As for the inevitable poverty of the old, labor force participation—the fundamental index of dependency—declined only marginally between 1890 and 1930. Although the number of children available to support the aged slowly diminished, the percentage of married people in the aged population increased, indicating broader distribution of an essential defense against dependency. Yet between 1920 and 1930 alone, the number of aged welfare recipients doubled. Neither the occupational nor the demographic status of the elderly (nor the combination of the two) explains these data. Indeed, since the number of *nonaged* recipients also rose rapidly, the manifest fact that the Boston Overseers became more generous constitutes the vital piece of evidence.

The sources of their generosity are not difficult to find. The historians Charles Trout and J. Joseph Hutchmacher, among others, have clearly established that the ascendancy of Irish political power in Boston, fully achieved by 1900, led to more liberal attitudes toward the disbursement of public funds.[20] Responding to ethnic, working-class voters, Irish politicians loosened the city's purse strings. These politicians appointed the Overseers and saw the welfare budget as one way to help their constituencies. The mayor had particular power over the budgets of municipal agencies. The dominant political leader in Boston in the 1920s was James Michael Curley, mayor in 1914–18, 1922–26, and 1930–33. Curley, who had grown up poor in an Irish slum in Boston, "liked to spend," and liked to spend for the poor: "I have known what it is to be hungry . . . , and if I have sometimes erred in response to the dictates of the heart rather than the head, perhaps I am not altogether to blame. . . . My sympathies and purse have been ever freely given to those who stood shivering in the shadow of adversity." A "popularizer of welfare on a grand scale," Curley represented just the attitude the Protestant welfare elite deplored.[21] Former Boston welfare officials vividly recall the struggles between the tightfisted Protestant social service officers and their Irish successors, who dispensed more aid and less social service.[22]

For the elderly the redefinition of deserving need had special meaning, since it undercut the threat of the almshouse and reduced reliance on children. Without generous outdoor relief, the poorhouse functioned to compel poor families to support their aged relatives. Clearly the worst alternative, the almshouse served, as its nineteenth-century founders intended, as a grim warning not to appeal to the public coffers.

By 1920 the men who directed Boston's public relief system were Irish Catholics elected and appointed by Irish Catholics. They sympathized with the plight of their fellow countrymen and countrywomen, just as the managers of the

Yankee private homes for the aged sympathized with their Protestant cousins and saved them from the almshouse. From the point of view of ethnic politicians, the working-class family struggling to raise children and care for feeble Aunt Bridget deserved help.[23] The corporation lawyers running the Yankee homes hastened to point out that the Overseers dispensed public money, raised from taxes on Yankee banks and businesses and from middle-class as well as working-class households. When the Overseers increased the number of aged beneficiaries and the benefit levels, taxes had to rise. The definition of "need" had direct economic consequences.

Throughout the 1920s, as the Overseers responded to their constituency by raising relief levels, advocates of state old age pensions, sensitive to the same population, demanded that the Commonwealth of Massachusetts transfer some of the common riches to poorer aged citizens. As in other states, the movement for old age pensions was a working-class movement, based in organized labor and dependent upon the ethnic communities that stood to gain the most when a general tax served a specific group.[24] Here, as the Massachusetts State Federation of Labor remarked in 1927, lay a subject "dear to the heart of all trade unionists."[25] By intensely lobbying Democrats and factory district Republicans in the state legislature, organized labor struggled to attach state revenues to provide welfare for the aged in working-class communities. In hearings held in Boston and other cities, politicians representing ethnic, working-class areas emerged as champions of pension legislation, and the referenda results from industrial towns indicated overwhelming support. The archdiocese of Boston, shepherd of the same constituencies in a city where 73 percent of the population was Catholic, strongly endorsed old age pensions, as did the state Democratic party.[26]

Proponents of state aid, representing lower-income groups, wanted liberal eligibility requirements and benefits and, always, a completely noncontributory funding structure. A noncontributory system was at the heart of this movement, and any scheme to fund pensions by taxing workers met stiff resistance. As might be expected, such proposals got a hostile reception, not least from the state Department of Public Welfare and its commissioner, Richard Conant. The latter, a creature and a captive of Boston's private welfare establishment, echoed that clique's attacks on the expansion of public relief, which came at the expense of punitive welfare principles, social service, and the pocketbooks of the native middle and upper classes.[27]

Like the rare progressive reformers whose rhetoric they borrowed, ethnic working-class leaders argued that old men and women could not survive in the modern world, and that increasing numbers found themselves impoverished in old age. They also asserted that workers found it impossible to save for old age while maintaining an American standard of living, and that a compensatory retirement wage was needed. They denounced the almshouse as a place that a decent family could never send an old relative.[28]

The first victory in this movement was the gradual expansion of city welfare; the second was the enactment of state OAA in 1930. Like the generous relief of the Boston Overseers, the state old age pension taxed all for the primary benefit of poorer families. Although local and state regulations forbade relief to the aged with relatives capable of supporting them, the breadth of OAA distribution in the city reveals the general disdain for such stipulations. In effect, both the Overseers and OAA *redefined* need to include older people who had families, a little property, or the capacity to work.[29] OAA nailed down a new right to assistance, relieved working-class families of some of the burden of support for the aged, and drew a retirement wage from the general treasury. The New Deal reinforced these accomplishments, backing them with the authority and largesse of federal revenues.

We err when we measure old age dependency by the numbers of older people receiving relief. The decision about what constitutes "deserving need" is intensely political and throws into conflict different interests in society. When we consider the demographic and occupational conditions in early twentieth-century Boston, the history of public relief for the elderly exposes the victory of one side in that social conflict. Those who got public aid in 1935 would not have qualified in 1895. Urban elders on relief in 1930 and 1940 and 1950 were not the victims of an inevitable force, the juggernaut of industrial development. They were the beneficiaries of a political victory and a new definition of the deserving poor.

Conclusion

This book set out to examine the troublesome issue of the social dependency of older people. Accustomed to view their decline as an unavoidable consequence of economic development, we have been warned in recent historical studies to examine instead the inexorable results of our culture's prejudice against old age. On the whole, the Boston case reveals milder economic effects than predicted, less prejudice than politics, and no inevitability at all.

Changes in economic structure surely affected older people. It is hard to imagine that the shift from farm to factory did not take a special toll on older Americans. Even those who remained on the farm lost their children to the cities, and with their progeny the rural elderly forfeited the matrix of respect and assistance that sustained them. But urban elders lost something more—that is, control of the means of production. Although rural life could be harsh and poorly rewarded, the rural aged often owned a farm and controlled their employment, its pace, and occasion; moreover, in the farm's tangible wealth, the elderly possessed an asset to use in bargaining for security when work was given up.

Urban elders worked for wages, renting out muscle and brain to the highest bidder. Some people chose this route because they had no capital for a farm; most took it because more money could be made in the city than in the country.

Before the welfare state, however, wage employment offered no guarantee of income when work was not available.

One of the themes of this book has been that work *was* available to older men, that they took advantage of the opportunities offered, and that they were not a dependent class. Even in jobs supposedly suitable only for the young, older men appeared in time and eventually assumed a proportionate place. Older women workers encountered greater obstacles because of their gender, but even their occupational record reflects this cohort effect. One of the most pernicious features of modernization theory—indeed, of any view that the welfare state was inevitable—is an implicit, vulgar ageism that assumes that older workers could not respond to the demands of industrial society. They could and they did.

Given that the average older man worked, what assets and liabilities did he bring to the labor market? Recent research indicates that older workers are valued by employers. They tend to be stable workers, with lower absenteeism, greater loyalty to the firm, and a reluctance to challenge management. Management's investments in training receive their returns in the employee's later years. If the job requires skill and experience, older workers can be very productive workers. Finally, the higher wages paid to senior employees, even when they are less productive, serve as a spur to productivity among younger workers, who see their eventual reward if they keep to the straight and narrow.

The Boston data suggest that many older workers of the early twentieth century possessed these attributes. Older men, well represented in stable and skilled occupations, eventually won a place in new fields. Since labor force participation and occupational proportion measure, however crudely, the well-being and independence of the aged, we should assume, until it is proven otherwise, that scholars have tended to exaggerate the poverty and dependency of older people before the New Deal. Even those older men not in the labor market were not all impoverished; in the growing American economy, some men could and did "retire." What New Deal welfare policies did was transform the normal pattern of work into the normal pattern of retirement. For this reason the New Deal should be seen less as a benevolent response to the needs of the aged and more as an active agent in producing their novel nonworking status.

Despite their command of certain assets, older workers also had significant liabilities. Older women suffered the consequences of gender: as wives they learned little that was valued in the labor market, and most widows had dismal occupational histories. Whether on the farm or in the factory, older men did not possess the physical strength of younger workers. Even in those occupations in which physical endurance meant less, the inability of very old or sick men to hold jobs cannot be denied. But the glaring weakness of older men was that they did not handle occupational change well. All their advantages depended on attachment to a particular job, skill, or employer. In a new occupation, older workers had no advantages of experience, promised little return on investment in training, and offered no greater loyalty to firm or managment. Whether we have found evidence of explicit ageism even in these instances of loss of security remains to be shown. Irrational prejudice against the old by employers—true ageism—should be distinguished from rational attempts to evaluate workers, however harmful these policies may have been to older workers.

Since economic development constantly induced changes in occupational criteria, it repeatedly challenged older workers. The form that such development took in the late nineteenth century probably had particularly deleterious effects. The rise of mass production industries meant the replacement of skilled workers, who had directed production, with semiskilled workers "scientifically" directed by management. This transformation led to a general degradation of skill in blue-collar work in the early twentieth century and diminished the opportunity of older workers to use experience and skill to retain their positions. The effects of these changes on older workers have not been studied. An inquiry into such effects would provide us with a better understanding of whether the twentieth century presented an altogether new challenge to the aged worker.

Yet right upon the heels of the transition from skill to scientific management came all the new devices—welfare capitalism, pension plans, personnel departments, and so on—signifying management's recognition that it had to promise new forms of security to replace the security once lodged in skill. In industries characterized by new production processes, management sought to retain experienced workers, to reduce turnover and keep loyal, stable employees, to moderate the unruly influence of young workers unaccustomed to the discipline of production, and to offer an assurance of steady wage increases to these youth if they accepted that discipline.

Nevertheless, some older workers did not retain their places. Some went out on strike, some got too old, or sick, or found themselves in obsolescent trades. As the experience of Boston women eloquently demonstrates, older women had very narrowly defined opportunities in the labor market, especially if they were widows with no training except in housework. Older men and women who fell out of the labor market came to depend on their families. The majority of these covertly dependent aged came from the poorer classes, and working-class immigrant populations in Boston bore the burden of support for many of the aged. The largest group among the covertly dependent were widows, who relied on their single and married daughters for boarding, lodging, and nursing care. These widows constitute that core of the "problem of the aged." As the ratio of children to parents declined, the probability that a child would have to support an aged parent rose dramatically.

Few alternatives to familial intergenerational support existed before the New Deal. Private and public institutions frowned on assistance to old people with children. In Boston lack of family was the key qualification for admission to an institution, whether an elite, ethnically discriminatory old age home or a public almshouse. Resistance to more liberal assistance (which might relieve the working-class family) drew strength from an old tradition in Boston. In the early twentieth century, however, the Irish came to dominate the city's public welfare system, and urban welfare became progressively more generous, including among its beneficiaries many of the city's elderly. The movement to provide still more money for the aged, based in the ethnic and class populations most likely to benefit from such relief, succeeded handsomely in Massachusetts. Driven by the specter of insecurity in their old age and the present need to provide for the old in their families and communities, working-class people sought a retirement wage for which all the classes would pay.

In the view of recent scholars, this movement coincided with the failure of businessmen to devise satisfactory private pension arrangments and with the efforts of the federal government to exert control over the national labor market. Thus, New Deal public relief programs reflected several influences. Designed in part to take older men out of the labor market, perhaps shaped by conservative elites within the state, these programs nonetheless breached an old line of defense against extension of public welfare. They supported very poor aged men and women regardless of family ties and they aided the widows of workers, even if the women had never earned a cent in "gainful employment."

In the creation of the welfare state, the working class won and lost. On the one hand, they got a substantial retirement wage. Aging parents could live in their own households, or the old mother could live alone, and we may infer from clear preferences today that both generations found these arrangements satisfying. In addition, older workers in ill health or tired of nerve-wracking, monotonous, or ill-rewarded jobs could quit work. Before the New Deal welfare system, many older workers could not afford to stop working whether they wanted to or not. After its institution, those trapped in inferior or degrading jobs could escape them, and the intermittently employed could leave the labor market. As benefit levels rose in the 1960s and 1970s, more and more workers found retirement a good alternative.

On the other hand, a fine old worker is a sight to see, and in retirement older people lost the dignity of work. They became dependent on the state and on a younger generation's whims and choices. Tranquility has not recently characterized the relationship between the aged and the young. A societal retirement system may easily set generations against each other and make older people vulnerable to the complaints of taxpayers. Greatly rewarded in the 1960s and 1970s, the elderly presently find less favor. The bulk of support for the elderly, once drawn from the general treasury, now comes directly from workers' paychecks, and workers with declining real incomes part with it reluctantly.

In the 1980s a triumphant conservative leadership actually concerned about the effects of taxes on initiative, thrift, and wage rates has encouraged taxpayers to believe that the Social Security system is not financially sound. What this elite has not explained is that every alternative has its costs. One way or another, old people must find financial support.

In the twenty-first century, older people will be, briefly, a large part of the population, an interlude in our course toward the mature demography in which a very high proportion of the American population will be of working age. Welfare programs for the elderly in this period will be expensive, but the alternatives impose penalties of their own. If the elderly return to the labor force, they will be competing for jobs, wages, and promotions, and in some occupations they will compete very well. In periods of high unemployment, their large presence in the labor force will have important effects on the availability of work and on wage rates.

Without a generous social security system, older people who do not work will often have to depend on their families, with the consequences revealed in this study. Many more families will find themselves facing very difficult decisions: whether to take older people in, how to provide nursing care, what resources to spend on aging parents rather than children. Social insurance, which spreads risk and provides families with more choices, has its merits.

Some middle course may be found. There may be a route that returns to older people the respect and independence gained in work, yet permits them to avoid the indignities of bad jobs and inevitable dependence on family members. This is the solution toward which our national intentions should be directed, but its achievement will require extraordinary inventiveness. The history of American old age is marked by three distinct periods: the preindustrial, industrial, and post-New Deal eras. It now awaits the fourth part.

Notes

Chapter I

1. Abraham Epstein, *The Challenge of the Aged* (New York, 1928), pp. 1–13.

2. Raymond Grew, "Modernization and Its Discontents," *American Behavioral Scientist* 21 (1977): 298–312; Daniel Lerner, *The Passing of Traditional Society: Modernizing the Middle East* (Glencoe, Ill., 1958).

3. Donald O. Cowgill and Lowell Holmes, eds., *Aging and Modernization* (New York, 1972).

4. A critical scholar can find every conceivable excess in modernization literature; another scholar could reproduce a theory with no flaws. My purpose is to recapitulate its consistent theses about aging in history. The sources from which my summary is drawn are: Ernest W. Burgess, "Aging in Western Culture," "Family Structure and Relationships," and "Résumé and Implications," all in *Aging in Western Societies*, ed. Ernest W. Burgess (Chicago, 1960); Margaret Clark, "The Anthropology of Aging: A New Area for Studies of Culture and Personality," *Gerontologist* 7 (1967): 55–64; "Cultural Values and Dependency in Later Life," in *Aging and Modernization*, ed. Cowgill and Holmes; Margaret Clark and Barbara G. Anderson, *Culture and Aging: An Anthropological Study of Older Americans* (Springfield, Ill., 1967); Lowell D. Holmes, "Trends in Anthropological Gerontology: From Simmons to the Seventies," *International Journal of Aging and Human Development* 7 (1976): 211–20; Richard A. Kalish, "Of Children and

Grandfathers: A Speculative Essay on Dependency," *Gerontologist* 7 (1967): 65–69; Robert J. Maxwell and Philip Silverman, "Information and Esteem: Cultural Considerations in the Treatment of the Aged," *Aging and Human Development* 1 (1970): 361–92; Margaret Mead, "Review of *Culture and Aging* by M. Clark and B. G. Anderson," *Journal of Gerontology* 23 (1968): 232–33; Erdman B. Palmore, "Sociological Aspects of Aging," in *Behavior and Modification in Late Life*, ed. Ewald W. Busse and Eric Pfeiffer (Boston, 1969); Erdman B. Palmore and Kenneth Manton, "Modernization and the Status of the Aged: International Correlations," *Journal of Gerontology* 29 (1974): 205–10; Talcott Parsons, "Age and Sex in the Social Structure of the United States," *American Sociological Review* 7 (1942): 604–16, and "The Kinship System of the Contemporary United States," *American Anthropologist* 45 (1943): 22–38; Talcott Parsons and Robert F. Bales, *Family, Socialization and Interaction Process* (London, 1956); Talcott Parsons and Gerald M. Platt, "Higher Education and Changing Socialization," in *Aging and Society: A Sociology of Age Stratification*, vol. 3, ed. Matilda White Riley and Anne Foner (New York, 1972); Michael Philibert, "The Emergence of Social Gerontology," *Journal of Social Issues* 21 (1965): 4–12; Irving Rosow, *Socialization to Old Age* (Berkeley, Calif., 1974); Leo Simmons, "Aging in Pre-Industrial Societies," in *Handbook of Social Gerontology: Societal Aspects of Aging*, ed. Clark Tibbitts (Chicago, 1960); *The Role of the Aged in Primitive Society* (Hamden, Conn., 1970); Keith Thomas, "Age and Authority in Early Modern England," *Proceedings of the British Academy* 62 (1976): 205–48; Clark Tibbetts, "Origin, Scope, and Fields of Social Gerontology," in Tibbitts, *Handbook of Social Gerontology*.

5. Peter Laslett, "Societal Development and Aging," in *Handbook of Aging and the Social Sciences*, ed. Robert H. Binstock and Ethel Shanas (New York, 1976); "The History of Aging and the Aged," in Laslett, *Family Life and Illicit Love in Earlier Generations: Essays in Historical Sociology* (Cambridge, 1977).

6. Erdman B. Palmore, *The Honorable Elders: A Cross-Cultural Analysis of Aging in Japan* (Durham, N.C., 1975).

7. Laslett, "Societal Development and Aging," and "History of Aging and the Aged."

8. W. Andrew Achenbaum, *Old Age in the New Land: The*

American Experience since 1790 (Baltimore, 1978); Thomas, "Age and Authority."

9. Achenbaum, *Old Age in the New Land*; David Hackett Fischer, *Growing Old in America*, expanded ed. (New York, 1978).

10. Pamela T. Amoss and Stevan Harrell, "Introduction: An Anthropological Perspective on Aging," in *Other Ways of Growing Old*, ed. Amoss and Harrell (Stanford, Calif., 1981); also see David Guttman, "Observations on Culture and Mental Health in Later Life," in *Handbook of Mental Health and Aging*, ed. J. E. Birren and R. B. Sloane (Englewood Cliffs, N.J., 1980); Thomas, "Age and Authority"; and Robert J. Maxwell and Philip Silverman, "Cross-Cultural Variation in the Status of Old People," in *Old Age in Preindustrial Society*, ed. Peter N. Stearns (New York, 1982).

11. Corinne N. Nydegger, "Family Ties of the Aged in Cross Cultural Perspective," *Gerontologist* 23 (1983): 26–31; Stearns, "Introduction," *Old Age in Preindustrial Society*, pp. 7–8.

12. Lutz K. Berkner, "The Stem Family and the Developmental Cycle of the Peasant Household," *American Historical Review* 77 (1972): 398–418; John Demos, "Old Age in Early New England," in *Aging, Death and the Completion of Being*, ed. D. D. Van Tassel (Philadelphia, 1979).

13. Fischer, *Growing Old in America*, pp. 76–78, 101–2, 109–13, 231.

14. Michel Dahlin, "Review of *Growing Old in America* by D. H. Fischer," *Journal of Social History* 11 (1978): 449–52; Lawrence Stone, "Old Age," in *The Past and the Present*, ed. Lawrence Stone (Boston, 1981); Achenbaum, *Old Age in the New Land*.

15. Quoted in James A. Henretta, "Mentalité in Pre-Industrial America," *William and Mary Quarterly* 35 (1978): 3–32.

16. Fischer, *Growing Old in America*, pp. 26–76, 82–86, quotation p. 52.

17. The power of property-owning elders in colonial America, a power that extended to the control of sexuality, can be reviewed in a rapidly growing literature: James W. Dean, "Patterns of Testation: Four Tidewater Counties in Colonial Virginia," *American Journal of Legal History* 16 (1972): 154–56; Philip J. Greven, "Family Structure in Seventeenth-Century Andover, Massachusetts," *William and Mary Quarterly* 23 (1966): 234–56; Philip J. Greven, *Four Generations: Population, Land and Family*

in Colonial Andover, Massachusetts (Ithaca, N.Y., 1970); Robert A. Gross, *The Minutemen and Their World* (New York, 1976); Alexander Keyssar, "Widowhood in Eighteenth-Century Massachusetts: A Problem in the History of the Family," *Perspectives in American History* 8 (1974): 83–122; Barry Levy, "'Tender Plants': Quaker Farmers and Children in the Delaware Valley, 1681–1735," *Journal of Family History* 3 (1978): 136–49; Daniel Scott Smith, "Parental Power and Marriage Patterns: An Analysis of Historical Trends in Hingham, Massachusetts," *Journal of Marriage and the Family* 35 (1973): 419–28; "Old Age and the 'Great Transformation': A New England Case Study," in *Aging and the Elderly: Humanistic Perspectives in Gerontology,* ed. Stuart F. Spicker, K. M. Woodward, and D. D. Van Tassel (Atlantic Highlands, N.J., 1978); and Michael S. Hindus, "Premarital Pregnancy in America, 1640–1971: An Overview and Interpretation," *Journal of Interdisciplinary History* 5 (1975): 537–70; Donald O. Souden, "The Elderly in Seventeenth-Century New England: Personal and Institutional Care in Old Age," paper presented at the Annual Meeting of the Society for the Study of Social Problems, New York, August 1976.

18. Dean, "Patterns of Testation," p. 170.

19. Smith, "Great Transformation," pp. 290, 296, citing John J. Waters, "An East Anglian Oligarchy in the New World," *Journal of Social History* 1 (1968): 351–70.

20. Smith, "Great Transformation," p. 296.

21. Henretta, "Mentalité in Pre-Industrial America."

22. Fischer argues that Whitman showed nothing but contempt for old age, but he does not review Whitman's complete works. Those pieces he does cite are misquoted and inaccurately dated, and his interpretation of them misrepresents Whitman's view of old age. For example, Fischer believes Whitman became progressively gerontophobic, but the poems cited were not written in an extended series but in a single period of ill health. Fischer fails to discuss Whitman's poems celebrating old age, such as "To Old Age" and "My 71st Year." On these points see Fischer, *Growing Old,* pp. 66–68, 119–20, 127 n. 13; Walt Whitman, *Daybooks and Notebooks,* vol. 2, *Daybooks, December 1881–1891,* ed. William White (New York, 1978), p. 453; ibid., *Collected Writings,* ed. Gay Wilson Allen and E. Sculley Bradley (New York, 1961); Gay Wilson Allen, *The Solitary Singer* (New York, 1967), pp. 527, 530–

31; Justin Kaplan, *Walt Whitman: A Life* (New York, 1980), pp. 12, 15, 31, 52–53, 345–49, 371–72.

23. Achenbaum, *Old Age in the New Land*, pp. 57–86.

24. Ibid., pp. 3, 9–37, 39–54.

25. Carole Haber, "The Old Folks at Home: The Development of Institutionalized Care for the Aged in Nineteenth-Century Philadelphia," *Pennsylvania Magazine of History and Biography* 51 (1977): 240–57; "Mandatory Retirement in Nineteenth-Century America: The Conceptual Basis for a New Work Cycle," *Journal of Social History* 12 (1978): 77–96; *Beyond Sixty-Five: The Dilemma of Old Age in America's Past* (Cambridge, 1983).

26. Thomas Cole, "Past Meridian: Aging and the Northern Middle Class" (Ph.D. dissertation, University of Rochester, 1980); Fischer, *Growing Old in America*; William Graebner, *A History of Retirement: The Meaning and Function of an American Institution, 1885–1978* (New Haven, 1980).

27. Howard Chudacoff and Tamara K. Hareven, "Family Transitions into Old Age," in *Transitions: The Family and the Life Course in Historical Perspective*, ed. Tamara K. Hareven (New York, 1978); Tamara K. Hareven and Howard Chudacoff, "From the Empty Nest to Family Dissolution: Life Course Transitions into Old Age," *Journal of Family History* 4 (1979): 69–83; Tamara K. Hareven, "Family Time and Historical Time," *Daedalus* 106 (1977): 57–70; "The Last Stage: Historical Adulthood and Old Age," *Daedalus* 105 (1976): 13–27.

28. Daniel Scott Smith, "A Community-Based Sample of the Older Population from the 1880 and 1900 United States Manuscript Censuses," *Historical Methods* 11 (1978): 67–74; "Historical Change in the Household Structure of the Elderly in Economically Developed Societies," in *Old Age in Preindustrial Society*; "Life Course, Norms, and the Family System of Older Americans in 1900," *Journal of Family History* 4 (1979): 285–98; also see Michel Dahlin, "Perspectives on the Family Life of the Elderly in 1900," *Gerontologist* 20 (1980): 99–107.

29. Smith, "A Community-Based Sample."

30. Ibid.

31. Dahlin, "Perspectives on the Family Life of the Elderly"; Smith, "A Community-Based Sample."

32. Smith, "Life Course," pp. 296–97.

33. Ibid.; Daniel Scott Smith, "Accounting for Change in the Families of the Elderly in the United States, 1900 to the Present," paper presented at the Case Western Reserve Conference on the Elderly in a Bureaucratic World, Cleveland, April 1983.

34. Abraham Holtzman, *The Townsend Movement: A Political Study* (New York, 1963); Roy Lubove, *The Struggle for Social Security 1900–1935* (Cambridge, Mass. 1968); Jackson K. Putnam, *Old Age Politics in California* (Stanford, Calif., 1970).

35. Achenbaum, *Old Age in the New Land*, chap. 7.

36. Ibid., pp. 57, 86.

37. W. Andrew Achenbaum, *Shades of Gray: Old Age, American Values, and Federal Policies since 1920* (Boston, 1983), p. 47.

38. As an instance, an author otherwise unsympathetic to Achenbaum's arguments: Graebner, *A History of Retirement*, pp. 10–14.

39. Achenbaum, *Old Age in the New Land*, pp. 66–75, 95–106, 183–84.

40. Brian Gratton, "The New History of the Aged: A Critique," in *Old Age in a Bureaucratic Society*, ed. David D. Van Tassel and Peter N. Stearns (Westport, Conn., forthcoming).

41. Alan Dawley, *Class and Community: The Industrial Revolution in Lynn* (Cambridge, Mass., 1976); Lee Soltow, *Men and Wealth in the United States, 1850–1870* (New Haven, 1975).

42. Stephan Thernstrom, *Poverty and Progress: Social Mobility in a Nineteenth-Century City* (Cambridge, Mass., 1964).

43. Kathy Stone, "The Origins of Job Structures in the Steel Industry," *Review of Radical Political Economics* 6 (1974): 61–97; Harry Braverman, *Labor and Monopoly Capital: The Degradation of Work in the Twentieth Century* (New York, 1974); Stephen Meyer, III, *The Five Dollar Day* (Albany, N.Y., 1981).

44. Chudacoff and Hareven, "Family Transistions into Old Age"; Dahlin, "Perspectives on the Family Life of the Elderly"; Michael B. Katz, *The People of Hamilton, Canada West* (Cambridge, Mass., 1976); Smith, "Life Course"; Soltow, *Men and Wealth*.

45. Graebner, *A History of Retirement*.

46. William Graebner, "Retirement and the Corporate State, 1885–1935: A New Context for Social Security," paper presented

at the Annual Meeting of the Organization of American Historians, New York, April 1978; *A History of Retirement*, p. 189.

47. Christopher Anglim and Brian Gratton, "Organized Labor and Old Age Pensions," *International Journal of Aging and Human Development* (forthcoming).

48. Brian Gratton, "The Virtues of Insecurity," *Reviews in American History* 10 (1982): 17–23.

49. The demographic, structural explanation for the rise of the welfare state can be found in Harold Wilensky, *The Welfare State and Equality* (Berkeley, Calif., 1975). John Myles, *Old Age in the Welfare State: The Political Economy of Public Pensions* (Boston, 1984); Jill S. Quadagno, "Welfare Capitalism and the Social Security Act of 1935," *American Sociological Review* 49 (1984): 632–47; Theda Skocpol, "Political Response to Capitalist Crisis: Neo-Marxist Theories of the State and the Case of the New Deal," *Politics and Society* 10 (1980): 155–201; Theda Skocpol, "Explaining the Belated Origins of the U.S. Welfare State," paper delivered at the Conference on Researching the Welfare State, Indiana University, Bloomington, Id., March 1983; Ann Shola Orloff and Theda Skocpol, "Why Not Equal Protection? Explaining the Politics of Public Social Spending in Britain, 1900–1911, and the United States, 1880s–1920, *American Sociological Review* 49 (1984): 726–50.

Chapter II

1. Unless otherwise indicated, census data used in the text and tables have been drawn from the following sources: Massachusetts, Secretary of the Commonwealth, *Abstract of the Census of Massachusetts, 1860, from the Eighth United States Census*, by George Wingate Chase (Boston, 1863), pp. 46, 315; U.S. Department of the Interior, Census Office, *The Seventh Census of the United States: 1850* (Washington, D.C., 1853), pp. 48–52; [Massachusetts Bureau of Statistics], *The Census of Massachusetts: 1875*, vol. 1: *Population and Social Statistics* (Boston, 1876), p. 223; idem, *The Census of Massachusetts: 1885*, vol. 1: *Population and Social Statistics*, pt. 1 (Boston, 1887), pp. 356, 430; U.S. Department of the Interior, Census Office, *Report on Population of the United States at the Eleventh Census: 1890*, vol. 1, pt. 2 (Washington, D.C., 1897),

p. 116; [Massachusetts Bureau of Statistics of Labor], *Census of the Commonwealth of Massachusetts: 1895*, vol. 2: *Population and Social Statistics* (Boston, 1897), pp. 414–15, 444; [U.S. Department of Commerce and Labor], Census Office, *Census Reports*, vol. 2: *Twelfth Census of the United States Taken in the Year 1900, Population*, pt. 2 [vol. 2] (Washington, D.C., 1902), p. 124; [Massachusetts] Bureau of the Statistics of Labor, *Census of the Commonwealth of Massachusetts, 1905*, vol. 1: *Population and Social Statistics* (Boston, 1909), p. 585; U.S. Department of Commerce, Bureau of the Census, *Thirteenth Census of the United States Taken in the Year 1910*, vol. 1: *Population: 1910* (Washington, D.C., 1913), pp. 298, 301, 331, 438; Commonwealth of Massachusetts, *The Decennial Census: 1915* (Boston, 1918), pp. 194, 305, 478–79; U.S. Department of Commerce, Bureau of the Census, *Fourteenth Census of the United States Taken in the Year 1920*, vol. 2: *General Report and Analytical Tables* (Washington, D.C., 1922), pp. 169, 289; idem, *Fifteenth Census of the United States: 1930, Population*, vol. 3, *Reports by States* pt. 1 (Washington, D.C., 1932), pp. 9, 14, 36, 1083, and vol. 2: *General Report* (Washington, D.C., 1933), p. 724; idem, *Sixteenth Census of the United States: 1940, Population*, vol. 2, pt. 3 (Washington, D.C., 1943), pp. 593, 670, and pt. 1, p. 22; idem, *Census of Population: 1950*, vol. 2: *Characteristics of the Population*, pt. 21: *Massachusetts* (Washington, D.C., 1952), pp. 39, 58, and pt. 1: *United States Summary*, p. 89. Subsequent citations will be in abbreviated form.

 2. Decline in fertility is the fundamental cause of increasing proportions of the aged in populations (see Ansley J. Coale, "The Effects of Changes in Mortality and Fertility on Age Composition," *Milbank Memorial Fund Quarterly* 34 [1956]: 302–7), but here we seek to understand the particular rapidity of aging in Boston after 1915. Jacob Siegel, while agreeing with Albert I. Hermalin ("The Effect of Changes in Mortality Rates on Population Growth and Age Distribution in the United States," *Milbank Memorial Fund Quarterly* 44, [1966]: 451–69) that immigration's net effect was to *retard* the aging of the American population, points out that heavy immigration prior to World War I "contributed greatly to the *rapid* increase in the number of persons 65 and over up to about 1960" (emphasis mine); Siegel and associates, "Demographic Aspects of Aging and the Older Population in the United States," U.S. Bureau

of the Census, *Current Population Reports, Special Studies*, series P-23, no. 59 (Washington, D.C., 1976), pp. 4–5, 12–13. For a discussion of immigration and migration to Boston, see Stephan Thernstrom, *The Other Bostonians: Poverty and Progress in the American Metropolis, 1880–1970* (Cambridge, Mass., 1973), pp. 9–28.

    3. *Census of Massachusetts: 1895*, vol. 2, pp. 447–48, 552–53; Conrad M. Arensberg and Solon T. Kimball, *Family and Community in Ireland*, 2d ed. (Cambridge, Mass., 1968), pp. 153–62.

    4. Oscar Handlin, *Boston's Immigrants, 1790–1880*, rev. ed. (Cambridge, Mass., 1959), pp. 239, 242, quotation on p. 12.

    5. David Hackett Fischer, *Growing Old in America*, expanded ed. (New York, 1978); Alton A. Linford, *Old Age Assistance in Massachusetts* (Chicago, 1949), pp. 5–17; Daniel Frank Detzner, "Growing Old Together" (Ph.D. dissertation, University of Minnesota, 1977); and Tamara K. Hareven, "Historical Changes in Major Life Transitions and in the Family," lecture given in the Humanistic Perspectives in Aging series, Boston University, 5 March 1979, Boston.

    6. *U.S. Census, 1850*, p. xc.

    7. *Census of Massachusetts, 1895*, vol. 2, pp. 704–7.

    8. U.S. Bureau of the Census, *Historical Statistics of the United States, Colonial Times to 1970, Bicentennial Edition*, pt. 1 (Washington, D.C., 1975), p. 15; Department of the Interior, Census Office, *Compendium of the Eleventh U.S. Census, 1890*, pt. 3 (Washington, D.C., 1897), pp. 180–83; *U.S. Census, 1950*, pt. 32, pp. 23, 189.

    9. See Massachusetts Commission on Old Age Pensions, Annuities and Insurance, *Report*, January 1910 (Boston, 1910), pp. 301–2, 308–10, 313–14, 322, 324–25, 329–30.

    10. *Historical Statistics*, pp. 15–18; *U.S. Census, 1950*, vol. 2: *Characteristics of the Population*, p. 177.

    11. *U.S. Census, 1940, Population: Nativity and Parentage of the White Population: Country of Origin of the Foreign Stock*, p. 93.

    12. For the timing of longevity advances for women, see Peter R. Uhlenberg, "A Study of Cohort Life Cycles: Cohorts of Native Born Massachusetts Women, 1830–1920," *Population Studies* 23 (1969): 416, and Siegel, "Demographic Aspects," pp. 12–

13. Imbalance in other cities can be noted in *Compendium of the U.S. Census, 1890*, pt. 3, pp. 181–83, and *U.S. Census, 1930*, vol. 2, table 33. For the excess of female immigrants in Massachusetts, see *U.S. Census, 1890*, vol. 1, pt. 1, p. xxii.

13. *U.S. Census, 1900, Population*, pt. 2, p. 124; *U.S. Census, 1940, Population: Country of Origin*, p. 85.

14. Robert W. Smuts, *Women and Work in America*, reprinted. (New York, 1971 [1959]), pp. 92–93, cites the New York *Tribune*'s stories; and see Leslie Woodcock Tentler, *Wage-Earning Women: Industrial Work and Family Life in the United States, 1900–1930* (New York, 1979), pp. 131–35.

15. *Historical Statistics*, pp. 20–21; Siegal, "Demographic Aspects," pp. 45–47; Uhlenberg, "Cohort Life Cycles," p. 411.

16. *Abstract of the Fifteenth Census, 1930*, pp. 254–55.

17. Howard Chudacoff and Tamara K. Hareven, "Family Transitions into Old Age," in *Transitions: The Family and the Life Course in Historical Perspective*, ed. Tamara K. Hareven (New York, 1978), pp. 224–27; Daniel Scott Smith, "Old Age and the 'Great Transformation': A New England Case Study", in *Aging and the Elderly: Humanistic Perspectives in Gerontology*, ed. Stuart F. Spicker, K. M. Woodward, and D. D. Van Tassel (Atlantic Highlands, N.J., 1978), p. 297; Peter Laslett, "The History of Aging and the Aged," in *Family Life and Illicit Love in Earlier Generations: Essays in Historical Sociology* (Cambridge, 1977), p. 201, table 5.10, and p. 202, table 5.11.

18. Tamara K. Hareven, "Historical Changes"; and Tamara K. Hareven and John Modell, "Urbanization and the Malleable Household: An Examination of Boarding and Lodging in American Families," *Journal of Marriage and the Family* 35 (1973): 469. Also see Matilda White Riley and Anne Foner, *Aging and Society*, vol. 1: *An Inventory of Research Findings* (New York, 1968), pp. 175, 180. As the conclusion of this chapter indicates, the abrupt decline of boarding and lodging for older people occurred after 1950.

19. *U.S. Census, 1940*, vol. 4, pt. 3, p. 3; *U.S. Census, 1950*, vol. 2, pt. 21, p. xviii. The latter source states that "as a result of this [definitional] change, the number of quasi households probably doubled in many areas." Total institutionalization among those 65 and over was 4 percent in 1960 for the United States and 7 percent

for Massachusetts. Ethel Shanas et al., *Old People in Three Industrial Societies* (New York, 1968), p. 21, and Barbara Bolling Manard, Cary Steven Kart, and Dirk W. Van Gils, *Old-Age Institutions* (Lexington, Mass., 1975), p. 63.

20. The correlation between institutionalization and lack of family ties is well known in contemporary social geronotology; see, for example, Peter Townsend, "The Effects of Family Structure on the Likelihood of Admission to an Institution in Old Age: The Application of a General Theory," in *Social Structure and the Family: Generational Relations*, ed. Ethel Shanas and Gordon F. Streib (Englewood Cliffs, N.J., 1965), pp. 163–87.

21. Interview with Sophia Loudon (pseud.), Dorchester, Mass., 2 May 1978. I conducted 20 interviews between February and May 1978 with persons 60–70 years of age who had lived most of their lives in Boston (no randomization was attempted, and the group may not be representative of their coevals).

22. Riley and Foner, *Aging and Society*, pp. 176–77; Erdman Palmore, "Total Chance of Institutionalization among the Aged," *Gerontologist* 16 (1976): 504–7.

23. Manard et al., *Institutions*, p. 125. The charitable homes discussed in Chapter IV compiled lists of acceptable boarding homes for their aged beneficiaries, and certain boardinghouse keepers were noted for their nursing.

24. For instance, Hareven, "Historical Changes."

25. Daniel Scott Smith, "Accounting for Change in the Families of the Elderly in the United States, 1900 to the Present," paper presented at the Case Western Reserve Conference on the Elderly in a Bureaucratic World, Cleveland, April 1983; Francis E. Kobrin, "The Fall in Household Size and the Rise of the Primary Individual in the United States," in *The American Family in Social-Historical Perspective*, ed. Michael Gordon, 2d ed. (New York, 1978), p. 76. Smith, while noting that more rapid changes have occurred since the Second World War, believes that attitudes about households shifted across the twentieth century and that this normative change affected families before the rise of the welfare state; see also his "Historical Change in the Household Structure of the Elderly in Economically Developed Societies," reprinted in *Old Age in Preindustrial Society*, ed. Peter N. Stearns (New York, 1982), pp. 265–66.

26. Smith, "Accounting"; see also Hareven, "Historical Changes."

27. A study done in the mid-1950s found that retired laborers were five times as likely as retired corporate executives to live with relatives outside the immediate family; John J. Corson and John W. McConnell, *Economic Needs of Older People* (New York, 1956), cited in an excellent treatment of the recent household experience of older people: Alvin Schorr, ". . . Thy Father and Thy Mother . . .": *A Second Look at Filial Responsibility and Family Policy* (Washington, 1981), p. 14. John C. Beresford and Alice M. Rivlin, "Privacy, Poverty, and Old Age," *Demography* 3 (1966): 247–58; Robert T. Michael, Victor R. Fuchs, and Sharon R. Scott, "Changes in the Propensity to Live Alone, 1950–1976," *Demography* 17 (1980): 39–56; Tamara K. Hareven and Howard Chudacoff, "From the Empty Nest to Family Dissolution: Life Course Transitions into Old Age," *Journal of Family History* 4 (1979): 76–77, 82–83; on the European family pattern, see Smith, "Accounting."

28. Fred C. Pampel, *Social Change and the Aged* (Lexington, Mass., 1981), pp. 157–71, 192–98; Kobrin, "Household Size," pp. 77–78; Boston interviews; Smith, "Accounting"; Daniel Scott Smith, "Life Course, Norms, and the Family System of Older Americans in 1900," *Journal of Family History* 4 (1979): 297.

29. Although certain items—e.g., food—may have been relatively cheaper in 1900, other items would be dearer; price indexes provide comparable measures of ability to purchase goods and services. Sources for these calculations are: *Historical Statistics*, pt. 1, series F 1–5, F 6–9, F 17–30, G 1–15, pp. 224–25, 289; Stanley Lebergott, *The American Economy* (Princeton, N.J., 1976), p. 5, n. 5, p. 321, table 1; see Smith, "Accounting," for the size of the middle class.

30. Alvin L. Schorr, *Filial Responsibility in the Modern American Family* (Washington, 1958), pp. 19–20.

31. Hareven and Chudacoff, "Empty Nest"; Smith, "Accounting."

32. W. Andrew Achenbaum, *Shades of Gray: Old Age, American Values, and Federal Policies since 1920* (Boston, 1983), pp. 42–43.

33. Kobrin, "Household Size."

34. Smith, "Historical Change," p. 266.

35. Smith, "Life Course," p. 294.

36. Smith, "Accounting"; Hareven and Chudacoff, "Empty Nest"; Smith, "Life Course," p. 296; Helena Znaniecki Lopata, *Widowhood in an American City* (Cambridge, Mass., 1973), pp. 114–23.

37. Kobrin, "Household Size," p. 78.

38. Boston interviews; also see Riley and Foner, *Aging and Society*, pp. 182–83. The contemporary preference of the elderly for separate residence has been well established in the social gerontological literature: Leopold Rosenmayr and Eva Kockeis, "Propositions for a Sociological Theory of Aging and the Family," *International Social Science Journal* 15 (1963): 410–26; Ethel Shanas, "Social Myth as Hypothesis: The Case of the Family Relations of Old People," *Gerontologist* 19 (1979): 3–9.

39. Kobrin, "Household Size," p. 78. The importance of demographic changes in reducing the ability of the family to support its aged members is discussed in Judith Treas, "Family Support Systems for the Aged," *Gerontologist* 17 (1977): 486–88. Alvin Schorr has stated the case for attention to structural population changes succinctly and well in "On Selfish Children and Lonely Parents," *Public Interest*, no. 4 (Summer 1966): 8–12. See also Siegal, "Demographic Aspects," pp. 55–56.

Chapter III

1. The reliability and validity of labor force statistics are discussed more fully in Brian Gratton, "Boston's Elderly, 1890–1950: Work, Family, and Dependency" (Ph.D. dissertation, Boston University, 1980), chap. 3. Labor force measures consider potential participation, not actual employment (i.e., they count both those who are employed and those who are looking for work in all censuses), and census takers took different views at different times of permanent unemployment, institutionalization, and so on. The aged may be particularly likely to report themselves as workers, although they may never be employed again. The change in the definition of the work force in 1940 can be traced in U.S. Department of Commerce, Bureau of the Census, *Fifteenth Census of the United States: 1930*, vol. 4, *Occupations* (Washington, D.C., 1933), p. 1; U.S. Department of Commerce, Bureau of the Census, *Six-*

teenth Census of the United States: 1940, vol. 3, pt. 3, *The Labor Force* (Washington, D.C., 1943), p. 3; U.S. Department of Commerce, Bureau of the Census, *Census of Population: 1950*, vol. 2, *Characteristics of the Population* pt. 21, *Massachusetts* (Washington, D.C., 1943), p. xxii; Alba M. Edwards, *Sixteenth Census of the United States: Population: Comparative Occupation Statistics for the United States, 1870–1940* (Washington, D.C., 1943), passim.

Durand's ratios can be found in his *The Labor Force in the United States, 1890–1960* (New York, 1948), p. 199, and see pp. 197–200. Definitional changes had their greatest effects among older age groups, but correcting ratios have not, to my knowledge, been developed for the urban population. Durand's ratios have been applied to the Boston data, however, to provide better and more *conservative* estimates than unadjusted census figures. Since the "gainful worker" concept inflated the LFPR of older men, extraordinary declines after 1930 in unadjusted data might be an artifact of definitional, not real, change.

2. As W. Andrew Achenbaum has pointed out, and studies of nineteenth-century LFPR confirm, participation rates of older workers cannot ever be expected to reach those of younger men; *Old Age in the New Land: The American Experience since 1790* (Baltimore, 1978), p. 67.

3. The quotation is from Durand, *Labor Force*, p. 34, but his opinion is shared widely. See Chapter I and discussion below on this point. David Hackett Fischer notes that LFPR in agricultural economies are usually spuriously high; see *Growing Old in America*, expanded ed. (New York, 1978), pp. 24–25, n. 41.

4. The assertion that the decline in LFPR did not begin until 1890 or 1900 is presumptive, and the evidence brought forth to support it can be shown to be internally inconsistent; Achenbaum, *Old Age in the New Land*, pp. 69, 183–84: Achenbaum's argument and data for twentieth-century decline can be found on pp. 95–106, table 5.6. Also see pp. 57–58, 86, and 203 n. 11. For problems in his nineteenth-century estimates, see Brian Gratton, "The New History of the Aged: A Critique," in *Old Age in a Bureaucratic Society*, ed. David D. Van Tassel and Peter N. Stearns (Westport, Conn., forthcoming).

5. Achenbaum, *Old Age in the New Land*, p. 102.

6. Brian Gratton, "Urban Labor Force Participation Rates,"

unpublished manuscript, Arizona State University, 1984. These data, derived from census materials, are available upon request.

7. Ibid. In regressions of urban LFPR on a variety of variables for 1890 and 1930, average wages had strong negative effects, indicating that some workers might be able to afford to retire.

8. Solomon Barkin, *The Older Worker in Industry: A Study of New York State Manufacturing Industries* (Albany, N.Y., 1933), pp. 289–305, presents a convenient summary of unemployment statistics before the establishment of New Deal programs. Barkin's analysis of the advantages of older workers is discussed below in this chapter.

9. Brian Gratton and Marie Haug, "Decision and Adaptation: Research on Female Retirement," *Research on Aging* 5 (1983): 59–76; Brian Gratton, "The Virtues of Insecurity," *Reviews in American History* 10 (1982): 17–23; Brian Gratton, "Labor Force Participation among Aged Males, 1890–1950," paper presented at the Conference on Researching the Welfare State, Bloomington, Ind., March 1983.

10. See Chapter VI for OAA in Massachusetts, and R. R. Campbell, *Social Security: Promise and Reality* (Stanford, Calif., 1977), p. 24, for the real value of the monthly benefit.

11. William Graebner, *A History of Retirement: The Meaning and Function of an American Institution, 1885–1978* (New Haven, 1980); Christopher Anglim and Brian Gratton, "Organized Labor and Old Age Pensions," *International Journal of Aging and Human Development* (forthcoming).

12. Marie Haug, Brian Gratton, and David Cogan, "Health and Women's Retirement Decisions and Adaptations," National Institute on Aging Project Proposal, 1983, section B; Gratton, "Virtues."

13. The liberal qualification standards for OAA in Massachusetts are described in Alton A. Linford, *Old Age Assistance in Massachusetts* (Chicago, 1949). Under the original Social Security Act, the tax on Old Age Insurance benefits could exceed 100 percent, since *any* wages received in "regular employment" would lead to a reduction in benefits "equal to one month's benefit"; Public Law no. 271, 74th Congress, H.R. 7260, section 202 (d). During the 1940s an amendment to the act allowed the beneficiary to earn up to $15 per month; Lewis Meriam. *Relief and Social Se-*

curity (Washington, D.C., 1946), pp. 107–8. Jill Quadagno reports that, because of pressure from southern congressmen, federal regulations did not prohibit states from giving OAA payments to persons making very low wages. Massachusetts did not permit such payments. See "Welfare Capitalism and the Social Security Act of 1935," *American Sociological Review* 49 (1984): 643.

14. Harry Braverman, *Labor and Monopoly Capital: The Degradation of Work in the Twentieth Century* (New York, 1974), pp. 282–83.

15. Sources for this summary of female LFPR, and for my conclusion that demand is the primary factor in recent LFPR increases, are: Valerie Kincaide Oppenheimer, *The Female Labor Force in the United States: Demographic and Economic Factors Governing Its Growth and Changing Composition* (Berkeley, 1970); Lynn Y. Weiner, *From Working Girl to Working Mother: The Female Labor Force in the United States, 1820–1980* (Chapel Hill, N.C., 1985); Alice Kessler-Harris, *Out to Work: A History of Wage-Earning Women in the United States* (New York, 1982); William H. Chafe, "The Paradox of Progress: Social Change since 1930," in *Paths to the Present: Interpretive Essays on American History since 1930*, ed. James T. Patterson (Minneapolis, 1975), pp. 5–55; Robert W. Smuts, *Women and Work in America*, reprint ed. (New York, 1971 [1959]; Durand, *Labor Force*, pp. 129–36; Karl E. Taeuber and James A. Sweet, "Family and Work: The Social Life Cycle of Women," in *Women and the American Economy*, ed. Juanita M. Kreps (Englewood Cliffs, N.J., 1976), pp. 31–60, quotation on p. 55; Hilda Kahne (with Andrew I. Kohen), "Economic Perspectives on the Roles of Women in the American Economy," *Journal of Economic Literature* 13 (1975): 1249–92; Linda Waite, "Working Wives, 1940–1960," *American Sociological Review* 41 (1976): 65–79; Robert E. Smith, ed., *The Subtle Revolution: Women at Work* (Washington, D.C., 1979); Glen C. Cain, *Married Women in the Labor Force: An Economic Analysis* (Chicago, 1966); Winifred D. Wandersee Bolin, "The Economics of Middle-Income Family Life: Working Women during the Great Depression," *Journal of American History*, 65 (1978): 60–74.

16. William Graebner, "Retirement and the Corporate State, 1885–1935: A New Context for Social Security," paper presented at the annual meeting of the Organization of American Historians, April 1978, New York.

17. For difficulties in comparing occupations across time, see U.S. Department of Commerce, Bureau of the Census, *Fourteenth Census of the United States Taken in the Year 1920*, vol. 4, *Population, 1920: Occupations* (Washington, D.C., 1923), pp. 10–13; Clyde Griffin, "Occupational Mobility in Nineteenth-Century America: Problems and Possibilities," *Journal of Social History* 5 (1972): 310–30; Gratton, "Boston's Elderly," chap. 3; and Edwards, *Comparative Occupation Statistics*, passim.

I have used Edwards' analysis to identify occupational titles with 95 percent comparability between censuses, and I note any instance in which deviation is greater than 5 percent. Before 1940 occupational categories included unemployed people; in 1940 and 1950, occupational data comprise only men and women actually employed.

18. Durand, *Labor Force*, pp. 110–12 and chart 8 on p. 111. Durand's analysis is, however, quite static, focused solely on the 1940 census.

19. The native birth and educational attainments more likely among younger women facilitated their acceptance into the new fields of clerical work. See Margery W. Davies, *Woman's Place Is at the Typewriter: Office Work and Office Workers, 1870–1930* (Philadelphia, 1982); Leslie Woodcock Tentler, *Wage-Earning Women: Industrial Work and Family Life in the United States, 1900–1930* (New York, 1979); Elyce J. Rotella, *From Home to Office: U.S. Women at Work, 1870–1930* (Ann Arbor, 1981). Miriam Cohen, "Italian American Women in New York City, 1900–1950: Work and School," in *Class, Sex, and the Woman Worker*, ed. Milton Cantor and Bruce Laurie (Westport, Conn., 1977), pp. 120–43.

20. A hint of such a prejudice is found in James W. Fisk, "Organization of Retail Selling Force," *Salesmanship* 4 (1916): 380, in which a survey indicated that age, next to previous employment, was the most important factor in selecting employees. Graebner, *The History of Retirement*, p. 44, argues that such bias was quite evident in early twentieth-century sales employment.

21. For an early example of a hasty evaluation of the aged worker's occupational opportunities, see Abraham Epstein, *The Challenge of the Aged* (New York, 1928), pp. 21–23, and, for a more recent one, Achenbaum, *Old Age in the New Land*, pp. 95–102, and pp. 99–101, table 5.5. Graebner's *A History of Retirement* is

also insensitive to cohort effects; see the discussion of printers below.

22. Graebner, *A History of Retirement*, pp. 21–25.

23. Lucille Eaves, "Discrimination in the Employment of Older Workers in Massachusetts," *Monthly Labor Review* 44 (1937): 1362. Or, as one man said of the senior hands in the factory in which he worked: "good old mold makers was hard to get." David Gaynor, interview, 6 March 1978.

24. Peter O. Steiner and Robert Dorfman, *The Economic Status of the Aged* (Berkeley, 1957), pp. 51–52.

25. Tamara Hareven, "The Last Stage: Historical Adulthood and Old Age," *Daedulus* 105 (1976): 20; Howard Chudacoff and Tamara K. Hareven, "Family Transitions Into Old Age," in Tamara K. Hareven, ed., *Transitions: The Family and the Life Course in Historical Perspective* (New York, 1978), p. 228. For this view of service trades in the 1920s, see Massachusetts Commission on Pensions, *Report on Old-Age Pensions* (Boston, 1925), pp. 62–63, and Barkin, *The Older Worker*, especially chap. 17.

26. Elliot Dunlop Smith, "Employment Age Limitation," abstract of discussions at a meeting of the eastern section of the Taylor Society, Boston, 5 April 1929, in *Bulletin of the Taylor Society* 19 (1929): 223–24, Barkin, *The Older Worker*, pp. 61, 143–57, 327–335, and chaps. 9–13; Graebner, *A History of Retirement*.

27. In a study of automobile workers and the seniority issue during the 1930s and 1940s, Carl Gersuny and Gladis Kaufman conclude that the senior employee reduced turnover and disciplinary problems, offering employers a number of advantages over younger workers; "Seniority and the Moral Economy of U.S. Automobile Workers, 1934–1946," *Journal of Social History* 18 (1985): 473. The relationship between length of service and productivity was well understood in the early twentieth century, when turnover in employment posed significant problems for management: "it is generally agreed that as the length of service of the employee increases, his value to the organization is also enhanced." Firms sought to retain "long-service employees," since their "cost of replacement" was high; Paul Frederick Brissenden and Emil Frankel, *Labor Turnover in Industry: A Statistical Analysis* (New York, 1922), pp. 115–16. Also see Arthur J. Todd, "Old Age and the Industrial Scrap Heap," *Journal of the American Sta-*

tistical Association 14 (1915): 550–66, and Stephen Meyer, III, The Five Dollar Day (Albany, N.Y., 1981), p. 99. Edward P. Lazear has connected higher wages for older workers specifically to mandatory retirement provisions, a recent observation which suggests the difficulties faced by early twentieth-century employers, and indicates why they experimented with private pension plans. See Lazear, "Severance Pay, Pensions, and Efficient Mobility," unpublished manuscript, University of Chicago and the National Bureau of Economic Research; the greater wealth of older men has been well established in the historical literature; see, e.g., Lee Soltow, Men and Wealth in the United States, 1850–1870 (New Haven, Conn., 1975). It is also likely that the older worker enjoyed a relatively high income, given the present practice of rewarding long-service workers. Evidence for higher income can be found in Barkin, The Older Worker, pp. 332–35, 339–47. Barkin's statistics on earnings from a variety of New York firms (2,102 firms and 364,000 employees) in 1930 consistently show wages rising by age, peaking in the thirties and forties, and then slowly declining. Since men in their fifties and sixties were more likely to own homes and to have fewer children to support, their relative income remained high. In my view, Barkin's comprehensive treatment, while unduly pessimistic, provides excellent evidence for the generally good circumstances of the majority of older workers, and the difficult ones of a large minority.

My primary source for the circumstances of older workers in recent decades is Herbert S. Parnes, ed., Work and Retirement: A Longitudinal Study of Men (Cambridge, Mass., 1981). Studies of the relationship between productivity and age are legion; for a convenient review, see David A. Waldman and Bruce J. Avolio, "A Meta-Analysis of Age Difference in Job Performance: An Addendum to Rhodes," paper presented at the meetings of the Gerontological Society of America, San Antonio, Texas, November 1984.

28. Eaves, "Discrimination"; Barkin, The Older Worker, pp. 61, 226–37, 255. Parnes, Work and Retirement, pp. 5–9, 65–92; and see "Loss of Job Hits Elderly Hardest," Cleveland Plain Dealer, 3 May 1982. For a general view of recent occupational trends among older workers see Thomas C. Nelson, "The Age Structure of Occupations," in Pauline K. Ragan, ed., Work and Retirement (Los Angeles, 1980); for the relationship of the older worker, obsolescent

skills and human capital or training, see Irvin Sobel, "Older Worker Utilization Patterns: Human Capital Approach," *Industrial Gerontology* 13 (1972): 6–28, and Gary S. Becker, *Human Capital* (New York, 1964) and "Investment in Human Capital: A Theoretical Approach," *Investment in Human Beings*, supplement, *Journal of Political Economy* 70 (1962): 9–49.

29. Since there were many single older women in Boston, and these presumably were more career-oriented and had more work experience, the lot of older female workers was, if anything, better in this city than in other populations.

30. Susan Benson, "The Clerking Sisterhood," *Radical America* 12 (March–April 1978): 41–55; Johanna Lobsenz, *The Older Woman in Industry*, reprint ed. (New York, 1974 [1929]), p. 39.

31. On differences between practical and trained nurses, see Susan Reverby, "Neither for the Drawing Room Nor the Kitchen: Private Duty Nurses in Boston, 1880–1914," paper presented at the meetings of the American Historical Association, San Francisco, December 1978.

32. Kessler-Harris, *Out to Work*, pp. 116–17.

33. Weiner, *Working Girl*, p. 87, for undercounting; Smuts, *Women and Work*, pp. 92–93.

34. For the similarities between housework and women's paid employment in this period, see Smuts, *Women and Work*, pp. 17–19; Rosalyn Baxandall, Linda Gordon, and Susan Reverby, eds., *America's Working Women* (New York, 1976), p. xv; and Tamara K. Hareven, "Modernization and Family History: Perspectives on Social Change," *Signs* 2 (1976): 200–202.

35. Davies, *Woman's Place*; Rotella, *From Home to Office*; Cohen, "Italian American Women"; Weiner, *Working Girl*.

36. Smuts, *Women and Work*. p. 52; Lobsenz notes the availability of domestic work for older women in *Older Woman*, pp. vii, 118. Tentler, *Wage-Earning Women*, pp. 131–35, provides interesting impressionistic evidence on the fate of older working women without families.

37. David M. Katzman, *Seven Days a Week: Women and Domestic Service in Industrializing America* (New York, 1978), pp. 87–91, for the timing of the decline in the participation of younger women. The transition to a day work system in domestic service may have favored older women (Weiner, *Working Girl*, p. 79).

38. For marital data, see [U.S. Department of Commerce and Labor], Bureau of the Census, *Occupations at the Twelfth Census* (Washington, D.C., 1904), p. 498; *U.S. Census, 1930*, vol. 4, pp. 755–56. The proportion of married women in these occupations also exceeded their average in the labor force.

39. A large literature attends these human capital issues. For women, and especially for the effects of marriage on their careers, see discussion in Kahne and Kohen, "Economic Perspectives." For examples of empirical research, see James Gwartney and Richard Stroup, "Measurement of Employment Discrimination According to Sex," *Southern Economic Journal* 39 (1973): 575–87, and Solomon William Polachek, "A Supply Side Approach to Occupational Segregation," paper presented at the Annual Meeting of the American Sociological Association, Toronto, August 1981.

40. Gratton and Haug, "Decision and Adaptation"; Gratton, "Virtues"; Haug, Gratton, and Cogan, "Health and Women's Retirement." See also Lowell E. Galloway, *Manpower Economics* (Homewood, Ill.: 1971), pp. 177–90.

41. Graebner, *A History of Retirement*, p. 53. For discrimination in the early twentieth century, see Lobsenz, *Older Woman*, pp. 56–59; Eaves, "Discrimination"; James J. Davis, "'Old Age' at Fifty," *North American Review* 225 (1928): 513–20, as reprinted in *Monthly Labor Review* 26 (June 1928): 1–6; and Barkin, *The Older Worker*. Yet each of these accounts has its ambiguities, and none proves pervasive ageism: that is, prejudicial discrimination based on irrational assumptions about the capacities of older workers.

Chapter IV

1. The origins of the two Homes, their leadership, and the connections between the founders and Boston's antebellum welfare reformers are closely examined in Brian Gratton, "Boston's Elderly, 1890–1950: Work, Family, and Dependency" (Ph.D. dissertation, Boston University, 1980), chaps. 4 and 6; idem, "The Boston Almshouse: 'A Reverence for God, the Hope of Heaven, and the Fear of the Poorhouse,'" paper presented at the meetings of the American Historical Association, Washington, D.C., December 1980. I have examined the antebellum welfare ideology in "The Invention of

Social Work: Welfare Reform in the Antebellum City," *Urban and Social Change Review* 18 (1985): 3–8.

In 1888, HAM officers explained the paradox of providing charity to the Yankees with one hand, while denying it to the Irish with the other, in this manner: "[The founders] realized that the vast influx from abroad, in consequence of the famine in Ireland, imposed a heavy burden on our public treasury, placing our own worthy poor at disadvantage, rendering it difficult to discriminate in their favor when they came to want. What would afford a reasonable support for our own aged and infirm, who had seen better days, and who were accustomed to more refined habits of life, would demoralize these strangers, weaken their incentive to effort, and reduce to pauperism"; HAM, *Twenty-Seventh Annual Report* (Boston, 1888), p. 7.

2. Brian Gratton, "Social Workers and Old Age Pensions," *Social Service Review* 57 (1983): 403–15.

3. HAW, *Thirtieth Annual Report* (Boston, 1880), pp. 5–6; Andrew Bigelow et al., "Memorial to the City Government," 26 April 1849, inserted in HAW, Minutes of the Meetings of the Board of Managers, meeting of 6 December 1849, Box 8, HAW Collection, Schlesinger Library; Massachusetts *Statutes 1849*, chapter 162. The name of the corporation was changed to the "Home for Aged Women" in 1872; Massachusetts *Statutes 1872*, chapter 297. For the directors' comments see Documents of the City of Boston, 1849, no. 19. For a more extensive discussion of the HAW, see Brian Gratton, "Labor Markets and Old Ladies' Homes," in *Older Women: Issues and Prospects*, ed. Elizabeth W. Markson (Lexington, Mass., 1983).

4. Henry B. Rogers, *Remarks Before the Association for Aged Indigent Females at the Opening of Their Home* (Boston, 1850), pp. 4–8, quotations on pp. 7–8. This pamphlet can be found in the bound volume of HAW annual reports (nos. 1–22), Box 3, HAW Collection, Schlesinger Library.

5. HAM, *First Annual Report* (Boston, 1862), p. 6; nativistic origins, overlapping leadership with the HAW, and links to Boston's elite are discussed in Gratton, "Boston's Elderly," pp. 158–64, 262–67. The HAW was never a women's association, though women participated in its founding and its by-laws required that at least a minority of the managers be female. The first woman

officer was not elected until 1878, and, up to 1950, no woman had ever filled the crucial offices of president or treasurer. See HAW, Minutes of the Meetings of the Corporation, meeting of 16 October 1851, Box 8, HAW Collection, Schlesinger Library; HAW, *Twenty-Eighth Annual Report* (Boston, 1878), p. 3.

6. HAW, Minutes of the Meetings of the Board of Managers, meeting of 18 July 1850. Also see minutes of the meetings of 25 April 1850, 16 May 1850, 30 January 1851 (here members note that money was given on the understanding that it was to be used for Americans), and 17 April 1851; HAW, *Second Annual Report* (Boston, 1852), pp. 2–3, 23. The early nativism of the managers can be traced in HAW, *Third Annual Report* (Boston, 1853), pp. 19–20; *Fifth Annual Report* (Boston, 1855), p. 9; *Sixth Annual Report* (Boston, 1856), pp. 11–12; *Twelfth Annual Report* (Boston, 1862), p. 33. The 1851 rejection can be found in HAW, Records of Inmates, 1850–1858, "Chiefly, cases not approved in Com^{ee}, or, rejected by the Board; or Names withdrawn:—" Box 11, HAW Collection, Schlesinger Library, and in HAW Minutes of the Meetings of the Board of Managers, meeting of 30 January 1851. G. Glover Crocker to Miss Addie Sears, 21 June 1921 and 2 November 1922, and passim, Correspondence of the Committee on Admissions, HAW Archives; for intolerance, see also HAW, Minutes of the Meetings of the Committee on Admissions, meetings of 20 January 1910 and 17 April 1912. For English parentage see G. Glover Crocker to Mr. Edward B. Richardson, 18 June 1924, Correspondence of the Committee on Admissions.

7. HAM, *First Annual Report* (Boston, 1862), p. 6; HAM, Minutes of the Meetings of the Corporation, Book no. 1, n.d., p. 5, petition dated 1 May 1860; HAM, *Fifth Annual Report* (Boston, 1866), p. 5.

8. HAM, *Eighth Annual Report* (Boston, 1869), p. 10. They added that "in the journey of life, disappointment and failure not unfrequently [sic] overtake the most ambitious and enterprising."

9. Massachusetts, Commission on Pensions, *Report on Old-Age Pensions* (Boston, 1925), p. 135; Gratton, "Social Workers."

10. The case records for the first HAW cohort, along with nineteenth-century records, are now deposited at the Schlesinger Library, Cambridge, Mass. Other case and administrative records remain in HAW Archives, Boston, Mass. Case records and other

HAM materials are held by the Rogerson House, Boston, Mass., and cited here as HAM Archives.

Cohort sampling was not random. In order to obtain the most complete information from irregularly complete files, all records in a continuous series were selected. For the HAW cohorts, the samples consisted of all the records for the following years: 1906–10, n = 67; 1925–29, n = 36; 1944–49, n = 77. Of these 180 records, 154 dealt with admissions and 26 with aid given outside the institution. An additional 45 records of applicants not aided were also reviewed. The HAM samples were drawn from 1906–09, n = 55; 1925–27, n = 34; 1942–49, n = 75. Of the 164 cases, 96 were awarded outside aid, often until admission to the Home could be arranged. Forty-five records of applicants not aided were also reviewed.

11. Case records described (with fictitious names) are no. 1098 (1900s) and no. 1093 (1900s), HAM. Christine McLeod (Secretary of Social Work) to Mrs. Harry Thompson, n.d. (1926), case no. 1717, HAM; HAM, Reports of the Committee on Beneficiaries, meeting of 5 December 1919; HAM, Reports of the Committee on Beneficiaries, meeting of 16 October 1922; case no. 2687 (1933).

12. HAW, *Fifth Annual Report* (Boston, 1902), p. 8. For New England subpopulations in Boston, see [Massachusetts Bureau of Statistics of Labor], *Census of the Commonwealth of Massachusetts: 1895*, vol. 1, *Population and Social Statistics* (Boston, 1896), pp. 132–39; vol. 2, *Population and Social Statistics* (Boston, 1897), pp. 671, 704–12; vol. 3, *Population and Social Statistics* (Boston, 1899), pp. 59–60, 174, 186; [Massachusetts] Bureau of the Statistics of Labor, *Census of the Commonwealth of Massachusetts*, 1905, vol. 1, *Population and Social Statistics* (Boston, 1909), pp. lxvi–lxix, 367–68.

13. Stephan Thernstrom, *The Other Bostonians: Poverty and Progress in the American Metropolis, 1880–1970* (Cambridge, Mass., 1973).

14. Rogerson to Donald Wilhelm, 18 January 1911, Rogerson Correspondence, HAM Archives. For the desire to serve those who had seen "better days" and the predominance of blue-collar beneficiaries in the nineteenth century, see Gratton, "Boston's Elderly," pp. 163–67.

15. Christine McLeod to George Crocker (Chairman of the

Committee on Admissions, HAW), 18 November 1922, Correspondence of the Committee on Admissions, HAW Archives; HAM, Reports of the Committee on Beneficiaries, report of 17 April 1925, HAM Archives.

16. These categories were chosen to fit the general patterns within the case records and followed in part those used by Stephan Thernstrom in *Other Bostonians*, appendix B, pp. 289–92. Thernstrom relied on Alba M. Edwards, "A Social Economic Grouping of the Gainful Workers of the United States," *Journal of the American Statistical Association* 27 (1933): 377–87.

17. The salaries of low white-collar workers in early twentieth-century Boston could be appreciably lower than the wages of skilled blue-collar workers. See Albert B. Wolfe, *The Lodging House Problem in Boston* (Cambridge, Mass., 1913), pp. 96–99.

18. Thernstrom, *Other Bostonians*, pp. 50, 110, 121, 142–44, tables 4.1, 6.3, 6.5, and Gratton, "Boston's Elderly," pp. 235–38.

19. Tamara K. Hareven, "The Last Stage: Historical Adulthood and Old Age," *Daedalus* 105 (Fall 1976): 20.

20. Caroline Hoppe and Judith Treas, "The Deserving Aged: A Los Angeles Retirement Home 1896–1930," unpublished manuscript, University of Southern California, 1980. Peter Stearns has also made this assumption; see *Old Age in European Society* (New York, 1976), p. 53. In recent work Hareven is more cautious. See Howard Chudacoff and Tamara K. Hareven, "Family Transitions into Old Age," in *Transitions: The Family and the Life Course in Historical Perspective*, ed. Tamara K. Hareven (New York, 1978).

21. Massachusetts Commission on Pensions, *Report* (1925), pp. 62–63.

22. Case no. 1097, 1900s cohort.

23. The sample of 29 was obtained by selecting every third case from 1850 to 1858 from HAW, Records of Inmates, 1850–1901, Box 11, HAW Collection, Schlesinger Library; the sample of 24 was obtained by taking every fifth case from 1861 to 1890.

24. Trained and untrained nurses could not be distinguished in the records, but these older women were not likely to have received formal training. At this time nursing duties were usually "an extension of the unpaid services performed by the housewife,"

having "more in common with domestic than professional service." The first quotation is from Gerda Lerner, "The Lady and the Mill Girl: Changes in the Status of Women in the Age of Jackson," *American Studies Journal* 10 (1969): 125, and the second from Robert W. Smuts, *Women and Work in America*, reprinted. (New York, 1971 [1959]), p. 74.

25. HAW, *Eleventh Annual Report* (Boston, 1861), p. 7.

26. Smuts, *Women and Work*, pp. 21–22, on nativity and white-collar work; Peter Filene, *Him/Her/Self: Sex Roles in Modern America* (New York, 1974), p. 29.

27. On pay scales see Ross M. Robertson, *History of the American Economy*, 3d ed. (New York, 1973), p. 382; for 1890 pay, see Smuts, *Women and Work*, pp. 89–93.

28. Interview with Mary Lee Westerhoff (pseud.), Boston, 17 April 1978.

29. The similarity of women's work inside and outside the home is remarked on by Smuts, *Women and Work*, pp. 17–19, and Rosalyn Baxandall, Linda Gordon, and Susan Reverby, eds., *America's Working Women* (New York, 1976), p. xv. Hilda Kahne (with Andrew I. Kohen), "Economic Perspectives on the Roles of Women in the American Economy," *Journal of Economic Literature* 13 (1975): 1263, notes that Juanita Kreps has maintained that, if so valued, housework would account for at least 25 percent of the GNP. The socialist argument can be found in Theresa Malkiel, "The Lowest Paid Workers," *Socialist Woman* 3 (1908), reprinted in Baxandall et al., *Working Women*, pp. 210–11.

30. No case number, 1900s cohort; case no. 903, 1940s cohort; case no. 934, 1940s cohort. As early as 1901 the managers commented on the difficulty older nurses had in obtaining employment; HAW, *Fifty-first Annual Report* (Boston, 1901), p. 10.

31. It is likely that their evaluations ignored equity in a home.

32. No case numbers, 1900s cohort; case no. 855A, 1940s cohort.

33. In the cross-tabulation of occupation with marital status, chi square was 31.4 with 6 degrees of freedom, significance = .000. Chapter III treats human capital issues for women.

34. David M. Katzman, *Seven Days a Week: Women and Domestic Service in Industrializing America* (New York, 1978), pp. 223–65.

35. Case no. 61, 1920s cohort.

36. Smuts, *Women and Work*, p. 23; National Manpower Council, *Womanpower* (New York, 1957), p. 134; U.S. Department of Labor, Bureau of Labor Statistics, *Labor Force Statistics Derived from the Current Population Survey: A Databook*, vol. 1 (Washington, D.C., 1982), pp. 708–9.

37. Female labor force participation is discussed in Chapter III; on the 1876–85 cohort experience see National Manpower Council, *Womanpower*, p. 127 and p. 128, fig. 3, and see p. 196, fig. 2, for an excellent graphic presentation of the curves of participation for 1890, 1940, and 1956.

38. An extensive literature has developed around the secondary, or "dual," labor market thesis. An introduction to this concept as it applies to women can be found in Alice Kessler-Harris, "Women's Wage Work as Myth and History: Review Essay," *Labor History* (1978): 287–307; Francine Weisskoff Blau, " 'Woman's Place' in the Labor Market," *American Economic Review* 62 (1972): 161–66. For a description of typical enterprises see Smuts, *Women and Work*, pp. 31–35, 104–9.

39. For example, Solomon William Polachek, "A Supply Side Approach to Occupational Segregation," paper presented at the annual meeting of the American Sociological Association, Toronto, August, 1981.

40. Case no. 63, 1920s cohort.

41. General Laws of Massachusetts, Chapter 273, Secs. 20–22; or Massachusetts Acts, 1915, chapter 163. This act made it a criminal offense for children to fail to support destitute parents. See the discussion of this statute in Alton A. Linford, *Old Age Assistance in Massachusetts* (Chicago, 1949), pp. 37–39.

42. That no child exist who could support an applicant was a conventional requirement of benevolent homes, as the 1925 Massachusetts report pointed out. Massachusetts Commission on Pensions, *Report* (1925), p. 138.

43. Cases no 1090 and 1105, 1900s cohort. Comparisons to surveys of Massachusetts poor old people in 1910 and 1925 confirm the finding that attenuation of family was marked among HAM and HAW clients. Massachusetts Commission on Old Age Pensions, Annuities and Insurance, *Report* (Boston, 1910), pp. 18–21, p. 59, table 1. Massachusetts Commission on Pensions, *Report*

(1925), pp. 41–43, 46–47, 54–55, 60, 70, 84, and p. 55, table 8. The latter report, using a very large sample, estimated that poor older men and women had an average of 2.6 children.

44. Case no. 1110, 1900s cohort.

45. The measure is suggested by contemporary studies of the relationship between distance and the support of kin; e.g., Bert Adams, *Kinship in an Urban Setting* (Chicago, 1968), pp. 38, 168–69. The low number of relatives is even more remarkable because most men were longtime residents of Boston, averaging 29 years of residence.

46. Case no. 846, 1940s cohort.

47. The proportion of single women aided rose from 30 percent in the 1900s to 40 percent in the 1940s, while the proportion of widows declined from 61 to 53 percent in the same period. This is in line with changes in the marital status of women in general and native-born women in particular. See Chapter II and Peter R. Uhlenberg, "A Study of Cohort Life Cycles: Cohorts of Native Born Massachusetts Women, 1830–1920," *Population Studies* 23 (1969): 407–20.

48. "The Effects of Family Structure on the Likelihood of Admission to an Institution in Old Age: The Application of a General Theory," in *Social Structure and the Family: Generational Relations*, ed. Ethel Shanas and Gordon F. Streib (Englewood Cliffs, N.J., 1965), pp. 163–87; quotation on p. 187.

49. Gratton, "Social Workers."

50. The first school is best represented by Tamara Hareven in her numerous publications and in her work as editor of the *Journal of Family History*; the second, by Christopher Lasch, especially in *Haven in a Heartless World: The Family Besieged* (New York, 1977).

51. Michael Anderson, "The Impact on the Family Relationships of the Elderly of Changes since Victorian Times in Governmental Income-Maintenance Provision," in *Family, Bureaucracy, and the Elderly*, ed. Ethel Shanas and Marvin B. Sussman (Durham, N.C., 1977), pp. 46–53; quotations on pp. 46 and 53. The strain of intergenerational dependency was certainly one motivation in the old age pension movement. See Abraham Epstein, *The Challenge of the Aged* (New York, 1928), p. 220. My interviews with older Bostonians strongly suggested the disharmony created when the generations depended directly on each other.

Chapter V

1. Isaac Rubinow, "The Modern Problem of the Care of the Aged," *Social Service Review* 4 (1930): 178.

2. This account is based on material from different periods: see the testimony of Dr. Simon Francis Cox in the "Majority and Minority Reports of the Committee on Institutions Departments Relative to the Investigation of the Boston Almshouse and Hospital at Long Island," *Documents of the City of Boston (DCB), 1903*, vol. 4, no. 102, pp. 1512–13 (also see p. 7); "Annual Report of the Institutions Department" ("ARID"), *DCB, 1896*, vol. 1, no. 14, p. 106; and "Annual Report of the Institutions Commissioner," *DCB, 1897*, vol. 1, no. 14.

3. Brian Gratton, "The Infant Geriatrics," *International Journal of Aging and Human Development* 19 (1984): 249–52.

4. Michael B. Katz, *Poverty and Policy in American History* (New York, 1983); Eric Monkkonen, *The Dangerous Class: Crime and Poverty in Columbus, Ohio, 1860–1885* (Cambridge, Mass., 1975); Brian Gratton, "The Invention of Social Work: Welfare Reform in the Antebellum City," *Urban and Social Change Review* 18 (1985): 3–8.

5. "Thirty-First Annual Report of the Board of Directors for Public Institutions," *DCB, 1888*, vol. 1, no. 13, p. 10; "First Annual Report of the Commissioner of Public Institutions," *DCB, 1890*, vol. 1, no. 25; "Annual Report of the Director of Public Institutions," *DCB, 1892*, vol. 2, no. 30, p. 31; "Annual Report of the Public Institutions Director," *DCB, 1894*, vol. 2, no. 29; "Annual Report of the Public Institutions Department," *DCB, 1895*, vol. 2, no. 29, p. 16; U.S. Department of Commerce, Bureau of the Census, *Paupers in Almshouses: 1910* (Washington, D.C., 1915), pp. 60–61.

6. For the legal definition of the almshouse, see Estelle M. Stewart, *The Cost of American Almshouses*, U.S. Bureau of Labor Statistics, Bulletin no. 386, June 1925, pp. 53–54. For complaints about indiscriminate mixing of populations, see "Twelfth Annual Report for the Boston Infirmary Department" ("ARBID"), *DCB, 1909*, vol. 2, no. 28, pp. 7–9.

7. Katz, *Poverty*; Monkkonen, *Dangerous Class*, p. 112; *Paupers: 1910*, pp. 9, 17–18; Eric C. Schneider, "In the Web of Class:

Youth, Class and Culture in Boston, 1840–1940," (Ph.D. dissertation, Boston University, 1980); Janet Golden and Eric C. Schneider, "Custody and Control: The Rhode Island State Hospital for Mental Diseases, 1870–1970,"*Rhode Island History* 41 (1982): 113–25; Peter Lawrence Tyor, "Segregation or Surgery: The Mentally Retarded in America, 1850–1920." (Ph.D. dissertation, Northwestern University, 1972); U.S. Department of Commerce, Bureau of the Census, *Paupers in Almshouses: 1923* (Washington, D.C., 1925), pp. 9–12.

8. An early reference to the aging of inmates in Boston's almshouses can be found in "Twenty-Ninth Annual Report of the Board of Directors for Public Institutions," *DCB, 1886,* vol. 1, no. 16, pp. 37–38. For Massachusetts data, see U.S. Department of the Interior, Census Office (Eleventh Census), *Report on Crime, Pauperism, and Benevolence in the United States,* vol. 3, pt. 2 (Washington, D.C., 1896), pp. 656, 784–89; and *Paupers: 1923,* p. 50.

9. W. Andrew Achenbaum, *Old Age in the New Land: The American Experience since 1790* (Baltimore, 1978), p. 80; U.S. Department of the Interior, Census Office (Eleventh Census), *Report on Crime, Pauperism, and Benevolence in the United States,* vol. 3, pt. 1 (Washington, D.C., 1895), pp. 286–90; *Paupers: 1910,* pp. 16–17, 89, and *Paupers: 1923,* pp. 9–10, 50; U.S. Department of Commerce, Bureau of the Census, *Historical Statistics of the United States*: Colonial Times to 1970, pt. 1 (Washington, D.C., 1975), pp. 15, 29; Stewart, *Cost,* p. iii.

10. Rubinow, "The Modern Problem"; Abraham Epstein, *Facing Old Age* (New York, 1922), p. 28; idem, *The Challenge of the Aged* (New York, 1928), pp. 33ff.

11. "Report of the Pauper Institutions Trustees," *DCB, 1899,* vol. 2, no. 25, p. 2; "Annual Report of the Pauper Institutions Trustees," *DCB, 1904,* vol. 2, no. 29, p. 7.

12. "Eighteenth ARBID," *DCB, 1915,* vol. 2, no. 16, pp. 6–7.

13. "Pauper Institutions Trustees," *DCB, 1900,* vol. 2, no. 28, p. 21. See also Adaline Buffington, "Francis Bardwell and the Future Care of the Aged," *Family* 10 (March 1929): 22.

14. Boston Finance Commission (BFC), *Reports and Communications,* vol. 11 (Boston, 1916), p. 86.

15. "Annual Report of the Pauper Institutions Department" ("ARPID"), *DCB, 1906,* vol. 2, no. 29, p. 4.

16. "Report of the Pauper Institutions Trustees," *DCB, 1899*, vol. 2, no. 25, p. 7.

17. [Massachusetts] Bureau of the Statistics of Labor, *Census of the Commonwealth of Massachusetts, 1905*, vol. 1: *Population and Social Statistics* (Boston, 1909), p. 585. For estimates of U.S. and Massachusetts almshouse populations, see note 9 above. In 1925 the Massachusetts Commission on Pensions reported that 1.8 percent of the state's residents 65 and over were in almshouses; *Report on Old-Age Pensions* (Boston, 1925), p. 37. The tendency of the aged to remain in the almshouse once admitted was regularly noted; see, e.g., [Massachusetts] Commission on Old Age Pensions, Annuities and Insurance, *Report* (Boston, 1910), pp. 36–38; Katz, *Poverty*, pp. 84–85.

18. *Paupers: 1910*, pp. 16–20; *Paupers: 1923*, p. 14; Katz, *Poverty*, pp. 122–23, 130. A study of Boston welfare in the 1920s concluded that aged women disliked the poorhouse, whereas "aged men" had "no feeling against going to an almshouse"; BFC, *Reports and Communications*, vol. 19 (Boston, 1924), pp. 166–67. Although more women than men are presently institutionalized, this is a function of their preponderance among the very old: unmarried men are notoriously susceptible to institutionalization; see Ethel Shanas et al., *Old People in Three Industrial Societies* (New York, 1968).

19. Sarah Orne Jewett, "The Flight of Betsey Lane," in *The Country of the Pointed Firs and Other Stories* (New York, 1954), pp. 179–80.

20. Within these case records, each category was arranged alphabetically: 3,223 deceased males (surnames B through Z); 2,234 deceased females (A through Z), and 1,137 discharged males (A through J).

Since the exact population of each group was known, sample sizes were determined for accuracy of estimation at ± 5 percent as follows:

$$\pm\ 0.05\ =\ 1.96\ \sqrt{\frac{p(1-p)}{n} \cdot \frac{(N-n)}{(N-1)}}$$

where p = percentage of attribute in group, using 0.5, which assumes the largest standard deviation; n = size of sample; N =

number 60 and over in group; solved for n. For this formula see Herbert Akin and Raymond R. Colton, *Tables for Statisticians* (New York, 1963), pp. 22–23.

Cohorts for deceased categories were determined by admission data as follows; 1908–18 ($n = 61$ for men, 124 for women); 1919–29 ($n = 102$ for men, 74 for women); 1930–40 ($n = 115$ for men, 70 for women), and 1941–51 ($n = 52$ for men, 33 for women).

Case records included the following information: name, age, place and date of birth, marital status, relatives, parents' birthplaces, occupation, religion, literacy, temperance, and penal record, as well as details of admission and subsequent disposition within the institution. The validity of the data recorded in the case records suffers by comparison with that of private welfare case records. Although police or city social workers sometimes verified information, in other instances the intake officer simply accepted the report of the inmate or a friend or relative. When the inmate lived at the almshouse for some time, the record generally contained more complete reports; for example, correspondence with children was noted. On the whole the records suggest that inmates had been known to city social workers or police in the community before commitment.

I have assigned case numbers to the records, and pseudonyms are used.

21. Confirmation of sample results can be found in the Massachusetts Commission on Pensions, *Report* (1910), p. 37, which stated that 92 percent of almshouse inmates 65 and over had entered after their sixtieth birthday.

22. I estimate that about one-third of the deceased group had some record of intemperance and/or a penal record. Intemperance was significantly correlated with number of admissions. A higher proportion of discharged males had deviant records.

23. Reports of the mid-1930s detailed the discharge of inmates able to secure outdoor relief; e.g., "ARID," *DCB, 1937*, vol. 1, no. 15, pp. 9, 15, 25.

24. For the claims of the medical staff see "Report of the Pauper Institutions' Trustees," *DCB, 1901*, vol. 2, no. 28, p. 5; "ARPID," *DCB, 1906*, vol. 2, no. 29, pp. 4, 12. The doctors found it useful to equate old age with illness: "their illnesses may be defined by no more special name than old age and general infirm-

ity"; "ARPID," *DCB, 1907*, vol. 2, no. 30, p. 9; see also Gratton, "Infant Geriatrics." For this tendency in late nineteenth-century medicine, see Carole Haber, *Beyond Sixty-Five: The Dilemma of Old Age in America's Past* (New York, 1983). Figures on hospital assignments at Long Island can be found in "ARPID," *DCB, 1905*, vol. 2, no. 29, pp. 32–33; "Twentieth ARBID," *DCB, 1917*, vol. 1, no. 5, pp. 31–32.

25. The disproportionately foreign character of national inmate populations appears in Census Bureau statistics: see *Paupers: 1910*, p. 9, and *Paupers: 1923*, pp. 21, 52. Boston nativity patterns can be found in U.S. Department of Commerce, Bureau of the Census, *Thirteenth Census of the United States Taken in the Year 1910*, vol. 1: *Population: 1910* (Washington, D.C., 1913), p. 438; idem, *Fifteenth Census of the United States: 1930, Population*, vol. 3, pt. 1 (Washington, D.C., 1932), p. 1083; idem, *Census of Population: 1950*, vol. 2: *Characteristics of the Population*, pt. 21: *Massachusetts* (Washington, D.C., 1952), p. 113 (20 percent sample).

26. Almost precisely the same ethnic patterns occurred in the sample drawn from the incomplete set of discharged men.

27. Discharged men exhibited similar occupational distributions; Stephan Thernstrom, *The Other Bostonians: Poverty and Progress in the American Metropolis, 1880–1970* (Cambridge, Mass., 1973), pp. 50, 115, 121, tables 4.1, 6.3, and 6.5.

28. Eric H. Monkkonen's study of the almshouse in Columbus, Ohio, from 1860 to 1885 provides support for this thesis. Monkkonen found more skilled blue-collar workers in the almshouse than unskilled and semiskilled combined. There was also a sizable proportion of white-collar workers. He also notes a decline in the proportion of inmates from the higher occupations across this period; *Dangerous Class*, pp. 143–47. Katz found little useful occupational data, but the Hoyt survey of New York almshouses in 1874–75 indicates large proportions of inmates had LBC backgrounds; *Poverty*, pp. 107, 125–26, 269.

29. Contemporary social gerontology emphasizes this correlation, but it was known during the early twentieth century. For a similar analysis of the significance of the family in institutionalization, see Pennsylvania Commission on Old Age Pensions, *Report* (Harrisburg, Pa., 1919), pp. 20–23, and Massachusetts Commission, *Report* (1910), p. 43.

30. At times the case record suggests that the agent took the name of one family member in order to contact the rest. Because of state laws requiring families to support their dependent members, paupers had a "well known" aversion to giving complete information about relatives ("Fourth Annual Report of the Institutions Registration Department," *DCB, 1901*, vol. 2, no. 19, p. 37). Nonetheless, the records specifically asked the number of children, and most listed several relatives, noting relationship to the client. The existence of a relative was no guarantee that assistance was available, as illustrated by the case of Charles Peglar (no. 0014), whose listed brother was reported as *"Not* interested."

31. The family networks of discharged men were even more attenuated than those of the deceased group. Men at the HAM reported an average of 1.4 relatives in Massachusetts, equivalent to the deceased almshouse group.

32. Case no. 0163, 12 October 1939.

33. Cohorts for women corresponded to those of men; see note 20 above.

34. "ARID," *DCB, 1921*, vol. 2, no. 14, p. 5. In January 1905, 18 percent of the almswomen 65 and over resided in hospital wards;"ARPID," *DCB, 1905*, vol. 2, no. 29, pp. 32–33.

35. *U.S. Census, 1910*, vol. 1, p. 438, *U.S. Census, 1930*, vol. 3, pt. 1, p. 1083; *U.S. Census, 1950*, vol. 2, pt. 21, p. 113 (20 percent sample).

36. Although foreign-born women were heavily represented in the national female almshouse population, especially in the more advanced age groups, the national proportions were lower than those found in the Long Island records. See *Paupers: 1923*, pp. 19–21.

37. Differences by ethnicity in time spent in the institution also suggest the custodial function of Long Island for Irish women, who tended to be long-term residents (chi square 20.04 with 10 degrees of freedom and significance = 0.0289). Although most immigrants moved to areas where relatives or friends lived, not all could. Single and widowed women, because of their marital status, were less likely than married women to have kin.

38. Frederick Bushee, *Ethnic Factors in the Population of Boston* (New York, 1903), pp. 92–3, quoted in Elizabeth Hafkin Pleck, *Black Migration and Poverty, Boston 1865–1900* (New York, 1979), p. 190.

39. Marital status effects, chi square 24.1, 9 degrees of freedom, significance = 0.004.

40. Mary Roberts Smith, *Almshouse Women* (Palo Alto, Calif., 1896), p. 26, quoted in Katz, *Poverty*, p. 123.

41. Chi square 26.794 with 15 degrees of freedom, significance = 0.0305.

42. Case nos. 720 (1916) and 924 (1919). In the latter instance a private charity apparently dictated policy to a public welfare facility.

43. Katz, *Poverty*, pp. 112, 130.

44. "Majority and Minority Reports of . . . Investigations," *DCB, 1903*, vol. 4, no. 102, esp. pp. 4–7, 113; "Annual Report of the Pauper Institutions Trustees," *DCB, 1903*, vol. 2, no. 20, p. 3. The quoted description, by almshouse officers, was made in the same year that Long Island was investigated by city authorities for abuses of inmates' rights by the medical staff.

Chapter VI

1. Interpretations of the origins of the American welfare state are discussed more fully in the conclusion of the chapter.

2. Charles H. Trout, *Boston, the Great Depression, and the New Deal* (New York, 1977), pp. 30–33.

3. "Annual Report of the Board of Overseers of the Poor," *Documents of the City of Boston (DCB)*, *1906*, vol. 2, no. 27, p. 3, and see "Annual Report of the Overseers of the Poor Department" ("AROPD"), *DCB, 1909*, vol. 2, no. 26, p. 11; Boston Finance Commission, (BFC), *Reports and Communications*, vol. 18 (Boston, 1923), pp. 181–82; BFC, *Reports and Communications*, vol. 19 (Boston, 1924), pp. 166–67. In 1925 the Massachusetts Commission on Pensions reported that among recipients of public outdoor relief in Boston who were 65 and over, 82 percent were females; *Report on Old-Age Pensions* (Boston, 1925), p. 105.

4. "AROPD," *DCB, 1918*, vol. 2, no. 21, p. 3.

5. The special funds aided 300 to 325 persons, most of whom were elderly, and were used in place of regular relief to avoid "wounding . . . delicate feelings" among the better class of pauper ("Inaugural Address of Nathaniel B. Shurtleff," *DCB, 1870*, vol. 1, no. 1, p. 9). In addition, I estimate that an equal number of aged

persons received "soldiers' relief," service-related pension programs funded by city and state. Brian Gratton, "Boston's Elderly,
1890–1950: Work, Family, and Dependency" (Ph.D. dissertation,
Boston University, 1980), pp. 365–72.

6. U.S. Department of Commerce, Bureau of the Census,
Fourteenth Census of the United States Taken in the Year 1920,
vol. 2: *General Report and Analytical Tables* (Washington, D.C.,
1922), p. 366; idem, *Fifteenth Census of the United States: 1930,
Population*, vol. 3, pt. 1 (Washington, D.C., 1932), p. 65.

7. The rapid increase in relief expenditure can be followed
in a graph of public relief costs in Boston from 1916 to 1929 in
Richard K. Conant, "Extent of Outdoor Relief," *Bulletin of the
Boston Council of Social Agencies*, 9 March 1930, p. 6.

8. BFC, *Reports and Communications*, vol. 18 (Boston,
1923), pp. 177–81, quotation on p. 177; BFC, *Reports and Communications*, vol. 19 (Boston, 1924), pp. 10, 166–67. Maurice Taylor, "Report on the Study of the Aged," 31 December 1926, p. 7,
in "Reports or Studies," HAM Archives, Boston, Mass. Christine
McLeod to Mrs. Corinne D. Marcesse, 12 March 1929, "General
Correspondence 30's–40's," HAM Archives.

In 1925 the Massachusetts Commission on Pensions reviewed outdoor relief to the aged in cities and towns in the state.
They concluded that "weekly aid amounting to $3, $4, or $5 per
person is common, but sometimes payments to aged persons run
as high as $7 a week or more"; *Report*, p. 100.

9. "AROPD," *DCB, 1917*, vol. 2, no. 21, pp. 1, 3, 9; "Fifty-
Seventh Annual Report of the Overseers of the Poor," *DCB, 1921*,
vol. 2, no. 18, pp. 1, 3; "Sixty-First Annual Report of the Overseers
of the Public Welfare (AROPW)," *DCB, 1925*, vol. 2, no. 19, p. 4;
"Sixty-Fifth AROPW," *DCB, 1929*, vol. 2, no. 23, p. 4.

Annual averages *underestimate* the grants typically received
by the aged. Calculated by dividing total expenditure by total number of cases aided, averages are reduced by high turnover among
younger recipients, who received aid for a short time but constitute
part of the yearly roll. The aged tended to remain on the rolls.

Nonetheless, the averages unmistakably reflect rising benefit levels. A slight deflationary trend in the 1920s meant that the
1929 average grant equaled about $288 in 1921 dollars. (However,
the 1917 grant amounted to $116 real dollars.) For cost of living

index, see U.S. Department of Commerce, Bureau of the Census, *Historical Statistics of the United States: Colonial Times to 1970, Part 1* (Washington, D.C., 1975), pp. 210–11.

10. Alton A. Linford, *Old Age Assistance in Massachusetts* (Chicago, 1949), pp. 85–87. Linford is the basic source for my discussion of Massachusetts OAA. Linford is of two minds about the extent of difference between this measure and previous forms (pp. 85–87 and 135–36). Like mothers' aid, OAA brought state participation, but, as is discussed in the text, this fact had limited effects on local policy.

11. Brian Gratton, "Social Workers and Old Age Pensions," *Social Service Review* 57 (1983): 403–15; Linford, *Old Age Assistance*, pp. 58, 88–89, 98–101, 125–34, 167–68, 250–56, 300–301, 409–19; Richard Conant, "Proposed Measures for Improving the Care of the Aged in Massachusetts," *Proceedings of the National Conference of Social Work* (1926): 562–64; Commonwealth of Massachusetts, *Annual Report of the Department of Public Welfare (ARDPW), 1924*, p. 3; idem, *ARDPW, 1925*, pp. 2–3; idem, *ARDPW, 1927*, p. 2. Conant argued before the legislature against an OAA law (Advisory Board of the Department of Public Welfare, *Minutes and Records*, 18 February 1927, p. 128, Archives, Commonwealth of Massachusetts). The animosity with which the Conant administration viewed OAA can be gleaned from the annual reports of the DPW in the early 1930s and from DPW, "Circular of Information," dated 8 June 1931, which was sent to local bureaus of OAA and can be found in "Pensions . . . OA Mass Public Documents and Regulations," Boston *Herald* Files, School of Public Communication, Boston University. Hostile sentiments can also be found in Advisory Board of the DPW, *Minutes and Records*, meetings of 19 December 1925, 19 February 1926, 19 March 1926, 18 February 1927, 1 July 1930, and 17 April 1935, Archives, Commonwealth of Massachusetts. Also see Martha Derthick, *The Influence of Federal Grants: Public Assistance in Massachusetts* (Cambridge, Mass., 1970), pp. 52–54.

12. Linford provides a very complete account of budgeting, minimum standards, and the gradual liberalization of benefits in *Old Age Assistance*, pp. 247–301.

13. See note 9 above for underestimation in average figures and cost of living index. OAA benefit averages more accurately reflect what an older person might receive in a year.

14. Linford, *Old Age Assistance,* pp. 109, 136–51, 176–246; *Historical Statistics,* pp. 210–11; Derthick, *Federal Grants,* pp. 52–53, n. 15, p. 252; "Eighty-Fifth AROPW," *DCB, 1949,* vol. 1, no. 23, pp. 10–12. Case records from the HAM confirm that the late 1940s monthly OAA benefit was about $60, or about $40 in 1931 dollars.

15. "Seventy-First AROPW," in *DCB, 1935,* vol. 1. no. 23, p. 39; "Seventy-Second AROPW," *DCB, 1936,* vol. 1, no. 23, p. 27; "Seventy-Third AROPW," *DCB, 1937,* vol. 1, no. 23, p. 3; "Seventy-Fourth AROPW," *DCB, 1938,* vol. 1, no. 23, p. 3; "Eighty-First AROPW," *DCB, 1945,* vol. 1, no. 23, p. 8; "Eighty-Second AROPW," *DCB, 1946,* vol. 1, no. 23, pp. 7, 11; "Eighty-Fifth AROPW," *DCB, 1949,* vol. 1, no. 23, pp. 5–6.

16. Linford, *Old Age Assistance,* pp. 169, 258.

17. The percentage on relief was calculated by estimating the caseload in 1920 as 1,250 and population 65 and over as 33,100; in 1930, 2,441 and 42,637; in 1950, 21,000 and 77,634. *U.S. Census, 1920,* vol. 2, p. 366; *U.S. Census, 1930,* vol. 3, pt. 1, p. 65; and U.S. Department of Commerce, Bureau of the Census, *Census of Population: 1950,* vol. 2; *Characteristics of the Population,* pt. 21; *Massachusetts* (Washington, D.C., 1952), p. 53.

In 1950, 225 of every 1,000 Americans 65 and over received OAA, and 225 received old age insurance benefits; Victor Christgau, "Old-Age, Survivors and Disability Insurance After Twenty-Five Years," *Social Security Bulletin* 23 (August 1960): 20–30. In 20 interviews I conducted with older Bostonians in 1978, nearly every respondent had known some family member who had gone "on the Old Age."

18. These interpretations are reviewed in Christopher Anglim and Brian Gratton, "Organized Labor and Old Age Pensions," *International Journal of Aging and Human Development* (forthcoming). As examples of the conventional historical view, see Roy Lubove, *The Struggle for Social Security, 1900–1935* (Cambridge, Mass., 1968); David Hackett Fischer, *Growing Old in America,* expanded ed. (New York, 1978), pp. 170–76; W. Andrew Achenbaum, *Shades of Gray: Old Age, American Values, and Federal Policies since 1920* (Boston, 1983), pp. 15–16, 37. For recent emphasis on the "state," state officials, and governmental structure (accompanied by de-emphasis of working-class influence), see Jill

S. Quadagno, "Welfare Capitalism and the Social Security Act of 1935," *American Sociological Review* 49 (1984): 632–47; and Ann Shola Orloff and Theda Skocpol, "Why Not Equal Protection? Explaining the Politics of Public Social Spending in Britain, 1900–1911, and the United States, 1880s–1920, *American Sociological Review* 49 (1984): 726–50; among the first Marxist analyses was Francis Fox Piven and Richard A. Cloward, *Regulating the Poor* (New York, 1971); more eloquent is William Graebner, *A History of Retirement: The Meaning and Function of an American Institution, 1885–1978* (New Haven, 1980).

19. Gratton, "Social Workers."

20. Trout, *Boston*, chaps. 1 and 2; J. Joseph Huthmacher, *Massachusetts People and Politics* (Cambridge, Mass., 1959); Peter K. Eisinger, "Transition to Irish Rule in Boston, 1884–1933: A Case Study," in *The Politics of Displacement* (New York, 1980). The Irish did not restrict their generosity to welfare. As many as one-third of the Irish families in Boston's West End neighborhood at the turn of the century were reported to have a family member with a political patronage job. Robert A. Woods, *Americans in Process* (Boston and New York, 1902), p. 121.

21. Trout, *Boston*, pp. 39–40.

22. I interviewed these officials in 1977, and most had participated in Boston and Massachusetts welfare politics in the 1930s and 1940s. They commented especially on the ethnic and class conflicts revealed in Richard Conant's replacement as state Commissioner of Public Welfare by Walter V. McCarthy. McCarthy, former head of the Boston Overseers, was appointed by Curley, who was governor of Massachusetts at this time. Similar controversy attended McCarthy's resignation under fire. The interviewees were Daniel I. Cronin (11 July 1977); former commissioner Robert F. Aut (12 July 1977); Richard Conant, son of former commissioner Conant (4 May 1977); Austin O'Malley, regional director, DPW (3 June 1977).

Martha Derthick also focuses on this period, noting that Curley's appointment of the Bostonian McCarthy ended the "Massachusetts tradition of nonpolitical, professionally oriented welfare commissioners." McCarthy did not get along with the (Protestant) private agency executives. *Federal Grants*, p. 27.

23. See Derthick, *Federal Grants*, p. 55. "That the elderly

poor deserve generous public support is a proposition with very strong moral as well as political appeal to legislators whose Catholic upbringing has imbued them with a strong sense of familial obligation to the aged, and whose life experience includes observation of widespread poverty among the older generations of their own stock;" As Robert Aut more succinctly put it: "The old Irish lady was sacrosanct" (interview).

24. Anglim and Gratton, "Organized Labor and Old Age Pensions."

25. Massachusetts State (Branch of the American) Federation of Labor, *Proceedings, Forty-Second Annual Convention (1927)*: 45.

26. Huthmacher, *Massachusetts*, pp. 186, 198; Trout, *Boston*, p. 21; Anglim and Gratton, "Organized Labor and Old Age Pensions."

27. Gratton, "Social Workers."

28. Anglim and Gratton, "Organized Labor and Old Age Pensions." The working class in England evinced a similar hatred of the poorhouse: see James H. Treble, *Urban Poverty in Britain, 1830–1914* (New York, 1979), pp. 105–6.

The opposition of pension advocates to contributory systems and their open efforts to secure a regular retirement wage follow precisely the general model of working-class efforts that John Myles has presented in his *Old Age in the Welfare State: The Political Economy of Public Pensions* (Boston, 1984).

29. Linford, *Old Age Assistance*, pp. 247–301; Derthick, *Federal Grants*, pp. 52–57; Cronin interview. The rigor with which lien laws, relatives' responsibility stipulations, and so on were enforced in OAA programs varied from state to state, Massachusetts being quite liberal.

Bibliography of Primary Sources

Manuscripts

Private Organizations

Boston, Mass. Boston Provident Association. Archives. (Held by the Family Service Association.)

Boston, Mass. Chancery of the Archdiocese of Boston. Archdiocesan Archives. Catholic Charitable Bureau Files.

Boston, Mass. Family Service Association (formerly the Family Welfare Society). Archives.

Boston, Mass. Home for Aged Men (now the Rogerson House). Archives.

Boston, Mass. Home for Aged Women. Archives.

Cambridge, Mass. Harvard University. Schlesinger Library. Home for Aged Women Collection.

Public Organizations

Boston, Mass. City of Boston. Department of Health and Hospitals. Long Island Hospital. Case records.

Boston, Mass. Commonwealth of Massachusetts. Secretary of the Commonwealth, Archives Division. Department of Public Welfare Collection.

Boston, Mass. Commonwealth of Massachusetts. State Library of Massachusetts. Incidental unpublished records.

Interviews

Boston, Mass. Twenty interviews conducted between February and May 1978 with respondents 60 to 70 years of age who had lived in Boston for most of their lives. Informed consent was given and pseudonyms assigned.

Griffith, Margaret. Home for Aged Women. Boston, Mass. Interview, 7 June 1977.

Lowy, Louis. Boston University School of Social Work. Boston, Mass. Interview, 28 March 1979.

Other Unpublished Sources

Boston, Mass. Boston University School of Public Communications. Boston *Herald Files*. File marked "Pensions . . . OA Mass Public Documents and Regulations."

Conant, Richard K. Papers. Milton, Mass. At the time of the study, held by Conant's son, Richard K. Conant.

Printed Records of Private Organizations

Home for Aged Men. *Annual Reports,* 1862–1950. Boston, Mass.

Home for Aged Women. *Annual Reports,* 1851–1933. Boston, Mass.

Society for the Prevention of Pauperism. *Annual Reports,* 1852–1861. Boston, Mass.

———. *Journal of the Society for the Prevention of Pauperism* 1 (April 1849 and February 1851).

Published Government Documents

Boston

Documents of the City of Boston. 1870–1951. Bound volumes containing the annual reports of the various city departments.

Massachusetts

Acts; Statutes. 1794, chapter 34; *1849,* chapter 162; *1860,* chapter 153; *1872,* chapter 297; *1915,* chapter 163.

Censuses of 1860, 1875, 1885, 1895, 1905, 1915.

Commission on Old Age Pensions, Annuities and Insurance. *Report.* Boston, 1910. Also available in Massachusetts House *Documents, 1910,* House no. 1400.

Commission on Pensions. *Report on Old-Age Pensions.* Boston,

1925. Also available in Massachusetts Senate *Documents, 1926*, Senate Document no. 5.

Department of Public Welfare. *Annual Reports, 1924, 1925, 1927, 1932.*

Department of Public Welfare. "Homes for the Aged in Ma." 18 May 1928. [Boston, 1928.] (Mimeographed.)

Department of Public Welfare. *Study of Local Infirmaries in Massachusetts.* N.p., 1945.

Finance Commission of the City of Boston. *Reports and Communications.* Vols. 1–45. Boston, 1908–1950.

Pennsylvania

Pennsylvania Commission on Old Age Pensions. *Report.* Harrisburg, Pa., 1919.

United States

Censuses of 1850, 1890, 1900, 1910, 1920, 1930, 1940, 1950, 1960, 1970, 1980.

Department of Commerce. Bureau of the Census. *Benevolent Institutions, 1910.* Washington, D.C., 1913.

Department of Commerce. Bureau of the Census. *Comparative Occupation Statistics for the United States, 1870–1940*, by Alba M. Edwards. Washington, D.C., 1943.

Department of Commerce. Bureau of the Census. *Historical Statistics of the United States: Colonial Times to 1957.* Washington, D.C., 1960.

Department of Commerce. Bureau of the Census. *Historical Statistics of the United States: Colonial Times to 1970.* Washington, D.C., 1975.

Department of Commerce. Bureau of the Census. *Paupers in Almshouses: 1910.* Washington, D.C., 1915.

Department of Commerce. Bureau of the Census. *Paupers in Almshouses: 1923.* Washington, D.C., 1925.

Department of Commerce. Bureau of the Census. *Special Reports. Occupations at the Twelfth Census.* [1900].

Department of the Interior. *Report on Crime, Pauperism, and Benevolence in the United States* [1890], vol. 3, pt. 2.

Index